To Daddy:

faithful Christian, loving father, and the funniest man I know!

Lee H. Holder

With special thanks to C.L.U.B. (Collierville Ladies

Understanding the Bible), a community Bible study that enriched

the pages of this book and this chapter in my life. Many thanks

for your rich insights and liberal doses of encouragement.

CONTENTS

INTRODUCTION

IN THE BEGINNING . . .

Eve introduced us to the wonders of womanhood: life itself, wifehood, and motherhood. She also ushered sin into the world with its accompanying curses of toil, pain in childbearing, and death. Sarah, in her willing submission to a nomadic life and in her belief that she could give birth even when past the age of childbearing (Hebrews 11:11), began a legacy of separation and faith that God used to grow a nation—a nation whose grandest triumph would be a baby in a manger, a Savior on a cross, and a risen intercessor on God's right hand. The dynamic of women in this eternal scheme of redemption is obvious. We saw in Genesis that God is able to accomplish His purposes by rewarding the obedience of women who are full of faith. But we also saw that He is able to use the deceit of Tamar or the seduction of Potiphar's wife to preserve the royal seed line of His Messiah.

God is able. His purposes will not be thwarted. *Women of Deliverance* begins with a courageous story of two Hebrew midwives who saved newborn babies from a powerful Pharaoh's death decree. One of those babies, saved from slaughter, grew up to be the greatest deliverer of Old Testament times—Moses. Women of deliverance used varying objects from a scarlet thread to a deadly hammer to achieve the purposes of God, but it was always God who put the power in the plan. God's preservation thread runs throughout this intriguing saga of deliverance and finally ties each episode to the cross.

Our lesson is glaring. God's will is a happening thing. We will not interrupt God's plan. We can be willing subjects in His divine scheme and be recipients of all benefits and rewards, or we can be unwittingly and perhaps unwillingly used as catalysts to accomplish His goals, mere pieces in His great puzzle. Either way, His will rules and reigns. Either way, He can use me whenever and however He chooses. In the latter scenario, I'm just His unwitting tool, forfeiting the rewards and the personal deliverance He has provided for me.

It is my prayer that those who study *Women of Deliverance* will be willing subjects of our God who is able. Great is His deliverance! (Genesis 45:7).

Chapter 1

Save the Babies!

The Hebrew Midwives

MIGHTY MIDWIVES

The book of the Exodus opens to find God's Israel in bitter circumstances of trial. Genesis closed with God's providentially placing the infant nation of Israel, consisting of only seventy souls, in the land of Goshen. This new environment isolated them from the idols of Canaan and gave them sustenance to become numerically strong.

The trouble for Israel began when a new king arose, a king who didn't recognize Joseph as the national hero he had been for Egypt as it faced the worst famine of its history.

Four hundred years had multiplied the seventy Israelite souls in Goshen to some two million people. The friendly, protective, pro-Israel kings had been dethroned by oppressive Pharaohs who were afraid that Israel would ally with some powerful foe in overthrowing the Egyptian dynasty. The solution for this royal insecurity was to crush the spirit of Israel using drastic tactics of oppression.

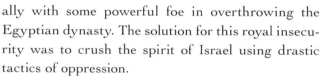

But the midwives feared God, and did not do as the king of Egypt commanded them, but saved the male children alive.

—Exodus 1:17

One of the king's first ideas was to do his oppressive dirty work through the Hebrew midwives, Shiphrah and Puah. These two busy ladies had undoubtedly shared the joy of birth with scores of Hebrew families. They were keenly aware of God's amazing phenomenon of birth. Imagine the terror that struck them as they appeared before the Pharaoh, arguably the most powerful man in the world at the time, and heard him say, "When you do the duties of a midwife for the Hebrew women, and see them on the birthstools, if it is a son, then you shall kill him; but if it is a daughter, then she shall live" (Exodus 1:16).

No doubt they exchanged horrified glances. Perhaps they thought of dear friends who were expecting babies. Perhaps they recalled precious newborn infants they had washed and wrapped in recent days. Whatever they were thinking, Scriptures give us no reason to believe they were thinking about obeying the king. Notice verse 17: "But the midwives feared God, and did not do as the king of Egypt commanded them, but saved the male children alive."

Exodus 1:6–8 describes a situation in which a king arose who did not remember the rich heritage of blessing brought to Egypt by Joseph and his trust in God. Write your feelings about leadership in an America that has largely forgotten our country's rich heritage we owe directly to adherence to biblical principles when our nation was born.

Our great country was founded on Christian principles – the further we drift from God, the less our nation is blessed + we have far more problems

What forms does Christian oppression take in our society?

NO PRAYER IN SCHOOL OR PUBLIC GATHERINGS
NO MENTION of GOD or JESUS

FEAR GOD

There are so many forces that we fear in our volatile society. I fear the force of Satan in the world in which my children will be raising my grandchildren. I fear the influence of my children's peers. I fear in smaller ways when I walk to my car as I leave the mall at night. I fear stock market recessions, tornadoes, and people with raging tempers. Unfortunately, even children have been forced to deal with the fear of terrorism in recent times.

The Pharaoh of Exodus 1 was a terrorist. Shiphrah and Puah were human. Of course they feared the power of the ruthless dictator. But they feared God.

The fear of God was not a terrifying sensation of being afraid. It was a deep respect for and awe of His power and majesty. Shiphrah and Puah were motivated by faith to preserve the children. There are potent lessons for those today who fear God.

PRESERVE THE CHILDREN

Abortion has claimed about one-and-a-half million lives per year since its legalization. In 1973, from a room in which several men in black robes debated life itself, a ruling emerged in the *Roe v Wade* case that stripped all rights from pre-born individuals. Since that time, we've learned that within a pre-born baby, all genetic material is complete at conception. We've gained access to technology that allows us to see within the womb. We now know that only twenty-two days after conception a baby's heart beats. At six weeks brain waves can be detected. At eight weeks every organ is in place. At eleven weeks the infant has fingerprints, a skeletal structure, a circulatory system, and nerves. Babies can experience pain at twelve weeks. All this happens in the first trimester!

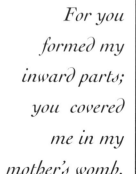

For you formed my inward parts; you covered me in my mother's womb.

—Psalm 139:13

We know that abortion stops a beating heart. How could any Christian woman, a woman who fears God, get her heart's consent to take human infant life? Shiphrah and Puah could not.

There are several methods of abortion. There is suction abortion, in which the infant is dismembered and then vacuumed from the womb. There is saline poisoning, in which the baby is forced to ingest a salt solution and begins to strangle and then dies over an hour later of acute salt poisoning. Today there are chemical abortions like the RU486 pill.

Consider for a moment the process known as partial birth abortion. Studies show that, as of this writing, only twenty-five percent of Americans are familiar with the process of partial birth abortion.

Take a moment to contemplate this process that, at the time of this writing, occurs daily in America.

A baby has developed almost, or even altogether, completely within a mother's womb. Partial birth abortions are performed only when the pregnancy has progressed past the twentieth week. (Recall how complete the anatomy is within the first twelve weeks.) Generally, all is physically well with both mother and child. The process of birth has actually begun. In many cases, the baby has been positioned so that tiny feet first emerge and little legs start to feel cool air for the first time. Then tiny fingers flex as they exit the canal and feel the cold air outside the womb. Then the doctor grasps the tiny body and positions the base of the baby's head so that he can insert a sharp instrument into the head at the base of the skull. As the stabbing occurs, the brain deflates, the skull collapses, and the dead baby is pulled from the womb.

As of this writing, this procedure is routinely occurring in our United States every day. Twice in the last few years our legislators have passed legislation banning partial birth abortion only to have that legislation vetoed by a pro-abortion President. At last, the legislation to stop this process has been signed by President George W. Bush. But lawsuits are occurring in all states that are effectively nullifying the ban on this life-saving legislation. It is as if thousands of innocent lives are struggling to make their way silently through the court systems of our lands until finally our Supreme Court will decide their fate. Christian women must be a voice for these lives. Those who fear God know that He is the one who covers life in the womb (Psalm 139:13). He is the one who forms pre-born life (Isaiah 44:2). Our voices can be heard when we write or call our legislators, when we write letters to news editors, and when we support with time and money pro-life organizations such as *National Right to Life* with its local chapters. Our most powerful voice is the one we raise in prayer.

> Brainstorm about things you can do in your community to protect unborn life. Are there volunteers to write letters to your newspaper and/or your legislators during the next week?
>
> _____
>
> _____
>
> _____

GOD'S PRESERVATIVES

We must also preserve the children in a spiritual sense. Women today save money in their own accounts and time by employing efficiently everevolving technology. They fight in the armed forces to save freedom. They are doctors who save lives and executives who save corporations. But, by and large, women in America today are losing their most precious and lasting commodity. We are losing our children. We lose them to materialism. We lose them to feminism. We lose them to immorality. In our materially driven pursuits we often leave them wandering in a sea of subjectivism and godless values that leave them powerless against a very real foe who is determined to win their souls.

Women in America today are losing their most precious and lasting commodity.

If we as Christian women are to preserve our children for the Lord we must fear Him. This awe and respect for Him must be bigger than all the Pharaohs of societal pressures, materialism, and selfishness that would smother the spiritual life of the next generation. Deuteronomy 6:2 begins with fear and ends with preservation of future generations: "That you may fear the Lord your God, to keep all His statutes and His commandments which I command you, you and your son and your grandson, all the days of your life, and that your days may be prolonged."

Deuteronomy 6:4–7 gives the keys to this preservation. Time and teaching are God's preservatives for our children. Whatever the price, we are called as mothers who fear the Lord to give our hearts, souls, and might to this process.

Read Deuteronomy 6. What specific guidelines are given to parents to help insure that our children and grandchildren walk in the ways of the Lord?

Teach them to love God & Keep His commandments

From Deuteronomy 6, make a list of the things God commanded in the accomplishment of this grand purpose.

Only serve God - Do not follow "other gods" - keep His commands, do what is right & good - remember & teach how God has delivered us from oppression

GOD MADE THEM HOUSES.

This phrase from Exodus 1:21 likely means that God blessed the midwives with children and physical blessings. God blesses us today when we commit to preserving the children. Parents who are willing to invest large amounts of quality time living Christianity before their children, and connecting all of the family's activities to Christ, will reap dividends of faith in future generations. But "unless the Lord builds the house, they labor in vain who build it" (Psalm 127:1).

The midwives were indeed women of deliverance in a dual sense. They delivered babies. Tiny, threatened lives were preserved because of their resolve. They also delivered Israel. Did you ever stop to think who would have delivered God's nation from Egyptian bondage if Shiphrah and Puah had destroyed that little baby Moses who later floated the Nile and parted the Red Sea? When I choose to go against the decrees of society around me and fear my God, I may not live to see the power of that decision fully manifested. But my God takes decisions of fear and turns them into His mighty deliverance in His own good time!

List some tangible blessings that I will receive if I successfully raise my children in the Lord. (Start with not having to worry about sexually transmitted diseases and progress to the privilege of praying together at family reunions. There are lots of big ones in between!)

unwanted pregnancies – lying – cheating – stealing abusing drugs

❧ *Cindy's Reflections* ❧

America at Auction

It was a bright summer morning and the small talk of the neighborhood could be heard as I meandered through the crowd that had gathered in the yard of the old home on the corner of Fifth and Madison. The old couple had been married for more than fifty years, but all of the laughter and love, trials and tears that were a part of this old home place had been reduced to an echoing memory. The porch was cluttered with the "stuff" of this now vacant house and the people, some who had known its inhabitants, some who were dealers in antiques, and some who were just curious about the goings-on of an auction were milling about and browsing through the musty smelling memorabilia-turned-merchandise. The clock had been ticking at the base of the big staircase for all of the old man's life and all of his father's and . . . well, now no one seemed to care. Dealers examined its old Seth Thomas label and tried to determine what it would bring. There were quilts that had been stitched at quilting bees in the old parlor and there was even one that had been a wedding gift to Great Grandmother, but it had been removed from the old rope bed in the guest room and thrown in a big pile of bed linens on the floor of the wooden porch.

At ten o'clock sharp, the gavel came down and the auctioneer began to chant. His call was intriguing and it was easy to become lost in his song and hardly even notice the items as they were sold, one by one, to the highest bidder. Wardrobes, dressers, watches, dishes, tools, washtubs, crocks, and hats with big boxes . . . all with numbers, sold to people with numbers, for dollar values. It all seemed such a thoughtless way for this old place to end. Yet the anxious bidders continued to nod with excitement as they anticipated taking home something that had caught their fancy.

The grandfather clock was different, though. At first, the dealers bid quickly against one another, until one by one they were eliminated. Finally, one of the bidders found himself bidding against an old white-haired lady who stood solemnly on the bottom porch step. As I glanced her way, astonished at her persistence in bidding against the wealthy dealer, I saw a tear roll down her cheek. Knowing then that the clock was more to her than an investment, I strolled over as she held up her number, relieved that her competitor for the prized clock had finally relinquished it. "You see," she said, "that's my father's clock . . . No price is too high."

Perhaps there are lessons to be learned from the Saturday morning auction that is a part of Southern Americana. I doubt that the couple who ambitiously worked, played, and raised their children in that old house ever seriously considered that one day the house and all of its contents would be listed on an inventory and sold to strangers. None of the members of this family would have ever considered selling out; not just a few years ago. But now things are different and it's a little easier, now that the old folks are gone. Its not so hard to watch the items go one by one, knowing that each one is bringing its fair price. Life is changing and so these remnants of another time are bartered one by one and with them goes the recollection of the way things used to be.

There's a sense in which we as Americans are witnessing an auction. It's a grand estate—this home we call America—and many sacrifices were made through the years to maintain it. It has weathered many a storm and has been a haven of freedom and happiness for generations.

Times are changing and those who built the house have long been gone. The "stuff" of this house is on the porch and the auctioneer is chanting to the crowd. One by one the "pieces" of this old home are placed on the auction block. Several of the most valuable and memorable items have already been sold and the prices they have brought have paled in comparison to their true value. Someone can recall a time when purity filled this old home, but alas, it has already been sold out to immorality. Fidelity was a foundational part of the house, but it has been replaced and so the auctioneer sold it cheaply. Hard work and its rewards have stood side by side in the house for generations, but alas, they too have been split into small lots and are being sold a little at the time. The Word of God was the centerpiece of this old dwelling. How many memories emerge from its use in this place! The children were taught daily from its pages and the family gathered around it each night before bed. For years, now, it has been unopened and forsaken on the shelf. Life without it just hasn't been the same. It was placed in a box and auctioned off as a box lot along with public prayer, the sacredness of marriage, the leadership of fathers, and the value of mothers in the home. Life is changing!

As a matter of fact, it is time for the bartering of life itself. Could it be that the value of life itself could be defined by a mere crowd of bidders gathered around the front porch? They are always there in every auction crowd . . . those who take no thought for the real intrinsic value of an item . . . those whose interest in the piece is merely mercenary. Could it be that no one who remembers where this life came from, the one to whom it belonged in the very beginning, will even enter a bid? Doesn't the thought of the real value of this precious article come to the mind of someone who recalls that it was the Father's gift even before this house was built? Which merchant in this thronging crowd can presume to know the value of this entity called life?

"What am I bid?" calls the auctioneer. As a tear rolls slowly down my cheek, I enter a bid from the steps of the porch. You see, this is my house. That is my Father's. And no price is too high.

"Thou hast granted me life . . ."

—Job 10:12 KJV

CHAPTER 2

MIGHTY MOM

JOCHEBED

THE MOTHER OF THE FIRST HIGH PRIEST

Jochebed, who is mentioned by name in only two passages, owns a place of honor in Israel's history because she mothered three great leaders in early Hebrew history. Her firstborn, Aaron, the original high priest and a gifted orator, spoke before the Pharaoh (Exodus 4:14–15), held the rod that turned water into blood (Exodus 7:19), and ministered in the Most Holy Place (Leviticus 16:2–3). His leadership abilities were so strong that he was able to guide Israel both in righteousness and rebellion (Exodus 32:3–4).

Jochebed delivered Aaron into a very hostile environment of unbelievable oppression. She likely feared for his young life, for it is probable that Aaron was born during the Pharaoh's terrorism of infanticide. Aaron survived the terror of the throne. But the throne couldn't survive the power God was to place in his rod.

So today, we as mothers cannot fathom the mighty works God may accomplish through the tiny babies in our wombs, then in our laps, and always in our prayers.

Since young children cannot read the Bible, drive to worship, or even formulate prayers alone, who is the connection between the small soul and its God?

THE MOTHER OF THE PROPHETESS

At the time of this writing my daughter, Hannah, is fifteen. She's growing up in a society gone mad over beauty, career, and money. If she picks up a teen magazine, she sees ads promoting sexuality and articles exonerating impurity. The icons of her peers are, for the most part, cheap and vulgar feminists. She has witnessed, via the media, the legal marriages of lesbian and homosexual couples. She lives in a world in which promiscuity is more common than abstinence among girls her age. One of my greatest joys during these precious teen years is traveling with Hannah and hearing her speak to groups of her peers about abstinence, modesty, and spirituality. I see the amazing power of God's guiding word reflected in her. It is when I hear her speak her convictions that I can perhaps most completely feel God's peace in this reveling society.

How proud Jochebed must have been if she lived to see the day when Miriam led her peers in the great song of deliverance following Israel's safe passage across the Red Sea. Her heart must have been swallowed in God's enveloping peace as she heard that song of praise: "Sing to the Lord, for He has triumphed gloriously! The horse and its rider He has thrown into the sea!" (Exodus 15:21).

Mothers cannot fathom the mighty works God may accomplish through the tiny babies.

THE MOTHER OF THE PRINCE

As exalted as Aaron and Miriam's place in Israel came to be, it was Moses who rose to a level of prominence unequaled in the annals of Old Testament history. In fact, no other nation has ever been so completely identified and historically tied to one man as was Israel with Moses.

Moses grew up in the palace. His deep faith in Jehovah, however, was not planted by the royal family, but grew in spite of his surroundings. It grew to these proportions:

- ❋ "By faith Moses, when he became of age, refused to be called the son of Pharaoh's daughter" (Hebrews 11:24).

- ❋ "Now the man Moses was very humble, more than all men who were on the face of the earth" (Numbers 12:3).

- ❋ "Not so with My servant Moses; He is faithful in all My house. I speak with him face to face, even plainly, and not in dark sayings; and he sees the form of the Lord" (Numbers 12:7–8).

- ❋ "And Moses indeed was faithful in all His house as a servant, for a testimony of those things which would be spoken afterward" (Hebrews 3:5).

✣ "But since then there has not arisen in Israel a prophet like Moses, whom the Lord knew face to face, in all the signs and wonders which the Lord sent him to do in the land of Egypt, before Pharaoh, before all his servants, and in all his land, and by all that mighty power and all the great terror which Moses performed in the sight of all Israel" (Deuteronomy 34:10–12).

From whence did such a deep and abiding faith come? We must surmise that it was cultivated largely by his mother, the nurse, who was likely his only connection during boyhood to his enslaved brethren and to the one true God.

Although Jochebed's name is not mentioned in faith's hall of fame (Hebrews 11), surely her personage is present: "By faith Moses, when he was born, was hidden three months by his parents, because they saw he was a beautiful child; and they were not afraid of the king's command" (Hebrews 11:23).

It was Amram's and Jochebed's faith that saw the baby Moses through the peril that was incipiently upon him. Faith hid the newborn, floated the infant, rescued the foundling, nursed the child, and nurtured the soul. God was clearly providing a deliverer, but His ark of safety for the baby was a pair of faithful parents; parents who were not afraid of the Pharaoh.

What actions can mothers take to help their children be leaders in fighting against these Pharaohs?

_____

_____

_____

Name and scripturally reference a time when each of Jochebed's children failed to be obedient.

_____

_____

_____

Why is it realistic to expect children to fail at times?

_____

_____

_____

HERITAGE OF FAITH

Can God still use faithful parents to nurture His leaders? More personally, can my prayerful parental determination instill the kind of character that chooses to "suffer affliction with the people of God" instead of engaging in "the passing pleasures of sin"? Can I pass along a faith that esteems "the reproach of Christ" greater riches than the "treasures in Egypt"? Jochebed witnesses that I can (Hebrews 12:25–26).

But I can't pass along a faith that I don't have. I cannot cower to the demands of the societal Pharaohs of the day—materialism, subjectivism, feminism, and political correctness—and still expect to raise a Moses.

Jochebed's success in instilling a faith in Moses, even as he experienced the elite and idolatrous lifestyle of the palace, is amazing. But when one examines the uncompromising nature of that faith, her success is even more striking. Moses never sat at the negotiating table with Pharaoh. He never considered making a deal of compromise. He never minced words. He never needed time to even think about Pharaoh's proposals. (Read Exodus 10:24–26.)

It has been my observation that uncompromising faith is generally both taught and caught. I can't merely make sure there is a Bible on my bedside table and that my child is in a weekly or bi-weekly Bible class and assume that he will absorb the faith. (Faith is not a liquid. It's a rock!)

I am convicted that it is only in attention to the details of my child's life—his obstacles, his conversations, his work, his play, his entertainment, and his education—that I can seize opportunities to build faith. When I'm in tune to God's will for my child and when I'm involved in the details of my child's days, that will of God has a way of permeating our activities. It is this constancy that fosters the faith of a Moses.

Cal Thomas said, "Children do not catch values the same way they catch a cold." Comment on the meaning and application of these wise words.

_____

_____

_____

"Education through permeation"—What does this phrase mean to parents who are working to instill faith in their children?

_____

_____

_____

⇜ *Cindy's Reflections* ⇝

God Bless My Baby

God give him strength as he enters our lives.
Give us wisdom as parents as each of us strives
To make for him places in our world to grow.
Teach us, Lord. We're so small. There's so much we don't
    know.

God bless him, as he to Thy wonders awakes.
Bless him, dear Lord, as his first steps he takes.
He's so small. May his scratches and bruises be small.
May a kiss "make it better" each time he may fall.

And help him to learn just what he should know
To take him, in life, just where he wants to go.
But in all of the learning, may he never forget
The One who has made him, and is keeping him yet.

Give him courage when Satan first gets in his way.
May he stay near Thy word. May he look up and pray.
May he put on Thee, Lord, is my most fervent prayer:
And, for all of his days, cast on Thee every care.

And when the time comes, that he must go away,
Help me to let go. But still I will pray;
God bless my baby, look down from Thy throne
And keep him from harm, for still he's my own.

Give him shelter, dear Lord, from this world's restless
    storm;
In a place where Your love shines . . . a place that is warm.
Give him people who'd help him keep You in his life.
Give him one of Your children, Oh Lord, for his wife.

And one day, may they know the joy I now feel
Of a life, yet unborn, but so precious and real.
May something I give him, while still he is mine
Make him know that the life, even unborn, is Thine.

So, Father, my prayer is for a life you're now giving
And yes, for a soul that will always be living.
My task is so great. I'm so small. Help me see
That through Christ I can do it . . . for He strengthens me.

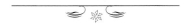

CHAPTER 3

OH BROTHER!
MIRIAM, THE PROTECTOR

A COURAGEOUS LOOK-OUT

The first portrait of Miriam shows her hiding behind the flags along the bank of the River Nile. She is vigilant in her duty to watch the little basket that floats among the flags, for inside the little ark rests her baby brother, ever in danger of being found and murdered by agents of the Pharaoh who is determined to squelch the growing Israelite population. We imagine the little girl amusing herself imaginatively, as little girls do, during the hours when the baby Moses is sleeping. We imagine her running to fetch her mother, Jochebed, when the baby awakens with a hungry cry. Perhaps she is running in response to such a cry when she first sees the entourage of the Egyptian princess. She stops cold in her tracks when she sees the maiden pull Moses' basket out of the water. We feel the helplessness with her as she hears the tiny cry from the ark now resting in the arms of royalty.

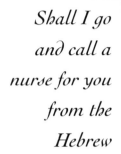

Shall I go and call a nurse for you from the Hebrew women?

—Exodus 2:7

Miriam was just a little Hebrew maiden. Some scholars believe she was between five and ten years of age. She could never have grasped the full import of the moment when baby Moses was winning the heart of the princess. She didn't know that this little ark was God's artillery against a powerful Pharaoh. This floating basket was God's battleship. The baby had literally been lifted in a slave-crafted basket to the lap of imperial luxury. Miriam was witnessing Israel's history in the making.

Important things were occurring that Miriam could not fully comprehend. But she did comprehend the meaning of the baby's cry. Moses needed his mother. Miriam responded insightfully, quickly, and with a spirit of ingenuity: "Shall I go and call a nurse for you from the Hebrew women, that she may nurse the child for you?" (Exodus 2:7).

And so Miriam, the little slave girl, had the courage to address royalty with an idea. It was this little girl's idea that kept Moses in touch with his Hebrew roots. It was this idea that gave Jochebed the space to nurse, but more importantly, to nurture the child. It was this idea that gave faith the fertile ground in which to grow inside Moses. The planting of faith resulted in decisions, deliverance, and a God-ordained destiny for Israel.

By faith Moses, when he became of age, refused to be called the son of Pharaoh's daughter, choosing rather to suffer affliction with the people of God than to enjoy the passing pleasures of sin, esteeming the reproach of Christ greater riches than the treasures in Egypt; for he looked to the reward. By faith he forsook Egypt, not fearing the wrath of the king; for he endured as seeing Him who is invisible. By faith he kept the Passover and the sprinkling of blood, lest he who destroyed the firstborn should touch them. By faith they passed through the Red Sea as by dry land, whereas the Egyptians, attempting to do so, were drowned (Hebrews 11:24–29).

The princess opened a basket. She delivered from death a baby. Her kiss turned him into a prince who would deliver from despair a nation whose Prince would deliver from death the whole world.

Baby Moses, lying in the princess' arms by the riverside, was to be extremely powerful as God's agent for delivery. But who did he need at that moment?

His mother

Who do babies always need for physical and spiritual nurturing to prepare them for God's purposes?

Mothers

What are some ways in which Christian women can be instrumental in restoring societal value to godly motherhood? Give passages of Scripture that admonish us to do so.

Give examples of contemporary families in which children have played a significant role in directing someone to the deliverance of Christ.

THE PROPHETESS

The intervening eighty-year period had been kind to Miriam. She had seen the mighty deliverance of Jehovah in an up-close and personal way. She had come to realize that within the little basket which she had guarded in the Nile had rested God's hand of salvation for the enslaved nation of Israel. She knew that God's care for Israel had been manifested through her as she ran to the princess and offered to find a nurse for Moses. She had come to realize that God can use what seems merely incidental to human eyes to accomplish His eternal purposes.

But, as is usually the case, Miriam likely had to pass through the fiery trial of suffering to fully know the mighty deliverance of God. She had witnessed the oppression of family members at the hands of cruel task-masters. She had likely wondered why God gave Moses a privileged protection amidst the riches of the palace while other family members knew only the tyranny of slavery. She had likely been amazed and saddened as she saw Moses forfeit this silver-spoon lifestyle to become a hireling shepherd. As forty years elapsed with no representation within the palace for God's suffering nation, her faith was likely tested.

But then came a day when both of her brothers went before the most powerful throne in the world and introduced Pharaoh to an infinitely more powerful monarch: the great I AM. What she witnessed in the upcoming weeks was incredible. She saw a river, the sustaining force of the great Egyptian nation, turn to blood. She marveled as a nation was brought to its knees by creatures of pestilence that consumed and violated. She looked from a lighted dwelling place to a land so black that human eyes could not penetrate the darkness. She had likely cooked the meat of a lamb and prepared unleavened bread as the lintels of her doorway were painted with the lamb's blood.

And then the incredible night came. A blood-curdling, collective wail arose from the Egyptian empire. Every household mourned the loss of its precious firstborn heir. The release of the slaves was immediate. They were thrust from the land so quickly that their bread was snatched up into kneading troughs and the troughs were bound into the clothes on their shoulders. The Egyptians, for once, were compliant, freely giving the Israelites articles of clothing, silver, and expensive jewels as they requested. Those who had forgotten the God of Joseph (Exodus 1:8) had been reminded of His omnipotence.

But a passion for vengeance filled the heart of Pharaoh. Realizing that He had lost his firstborn son, he regretted having released them. The Lord hardened his heart and, with all of his militia, Pharaoh pursued Israel. He fully intended to overtake, overcome, and overpower them, forcing them back under his oppressive hand.

The scene is the western shore of the Red Sea. The Israelites looked back over the well-watered plain they had traversed since their emergency exodus from Goshen. Imagine their horror as they saw on the western horizon a cloud of dust. Then they began to hear the thunder of the hoofs of an army. It began to seem apparent that they were being pursued. No doubt mothers wept as they hugged their babies. Fathers began to look for hiding places. But there was no time to run. They were a huge and obvious assembly of men, women, and children in a wide open plain of vulnerability. Amidst the wailing, voices of dissension began to grow among the people.

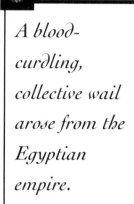

A blood-curdling, collective wail arose from the Egyptian empire.

> Then they said to Moses, "Because there were no graves in Egypt, have you taken us away to die in the wilderness? Why have you so dealt with us, to bring us up out of Egypt? Is this not the word that we told you in Egypt, saying, 'Let us alone that we may serve the Egyptians'? For it would have been better for us to serve the Egyptians than that we should die in the wilderness" (Exodus 14:11–12).

Miriam, who had protected Moses when endangered by the Pharaoh as an infant, stood by helplessly this time, no doubt wondering how God would deliver in this seemingly hopeless scenario. But imagine her wonder as she heard the faith-filled response of Moses:

> Do not be afraid. Stand still, and see the salvation of the Lord, which He will accomplish for you today. For the Egyptians whom you see today, you shall see again no more forever. The Lord will fight for you, and you shall hold your peace (Exodus 14:13–14).

Then she saw the great salvation of the Almighty. She stepped in faith into the bed of the sea and triumphantly marched across and up the eastern bank to turn and see the armies—horsemen, chariots, and even Pharaoh himself—crushed in the mighty collapse of the waters that had been walls of fortress for her people.

And then comes the song of deliverance. The expression of triumphant faith has always been a song. Heaven will raise a song of triumph for all of eternity. Exodus 15 is the earliest recorded Hebrew song of praise. Miriam, now described as a prophetess, one who received revelations from God Himself (Numbers 12:6), with jubilant dancing and song answered the song of Israel with these words: "Sing to the Lord, for He has triumphed gloriously! The horse and its rider He has thrown into the sea!" (Exodus 15:21).

She was a prophetess of praise. Should we as Christian women be any less joyful about our great deliverance today? Surely our revelation through the Holy Scriptures is an even greater treasure than the visions given to Miriam. Surely our deliverance from sin is infinitely greater than the escape from Pharaoh; yet how often our response is a sigh rather than a song. We should be joyful and let the world know the source of our joy.

List five unexpected blessings of the day for which you can offer praise and thanksgiving.

_____

_____

_____

_____

_____

_____

God blesses us beyond what we even can ask or imagine, as you have learned from the above exercise. Find a passage that says He is able to bless in this way.

_____

_____

THE PROUD ONE

Sadly, somewhere between the banks of the Red Sea and the encampment at Hazeroth, a deep resentment grew in Miriam's heart. Moses had married an Ethiopian woman. Whether or not Miriam had any real cause to dislike her new sister-in-law, we do not know. We know that God had placed no marital prohibition relative to the Ethiopians as he had relative to the nations of Canaan. (See Exodus 34:10–16.) Although the Scriptures say that Miriam and Aaron spoke against Moses because of the Cushite (Ethiopian) woman, perhaps this union was only the proverbial straw that broke the camel's back. It appears that Miriam had allowed a resentment to build within her spirit toward Moses. She and Aaron spoke against Jehovah's chosen leader, seemingly attempting to claim some of his greatness for themselves. God had selected Aaron as Moses' spokesman before Pharaoh and as the holy high priest of God. He should have been humbled by God's blessings of leadership. Miriam, a prophetess, was blessed with personal revelations from heaven. She led the women in praise. No doubt she was highly esteemed by the women of Israel. But praise has been replaced by pride. She apparently coveted the face-to-face relationship enjoyed only by Moses.

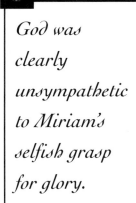

God was clearly unsympathetic to Miriam's selfish grasp for glory.

God was clearly unsympathetic to Miriam's selfish grasp for glory. She had dared to speak against God's meekest servant (Numbers 12:3); the one with whom He directly spoke face to face (v. 8); the only one who sees the form of the Lord (v. 8). The Lord took Miriam's insult as a brazen personal assault toward heaven, indeed so serious that He called the three siblings to gather before Him.

Imagine the fear and trembling that Miriam must have experienced as she made her way to the tabernacle of the Most High. As I try to feel her dread, my palms become sweaty and I get a nauseous anxiety. But even in her apprehension, she could never have imagined the terror of His rebuke.

When the meeting was over and the cloud lifted, Miriam was leprous—white as snow. She was incurably ill, extremely contagious, and painfully aware that Moses was God's chosen leader. Sometimes God allows our circumstances to cultivate certain character traits over time. But in this case, he gave Miriam instant humility. Her skin manifested God's displeasure for all to see. The nation stood still, halting its march to Canaan for a full week. Everyone was aware that the delay was due to Miriam's sin. It is clear from verse 14 that God's purpose was to make her ashamed. Even as Aaron repented and Moses cried out to God for her healing, Jehovah insisted on this week of intense humbling for Miriam.

List two Scripture references that instruct the Christian in her relationship to elders.

1. _____ 2. _____

Compare these references with God's statements in Numbers 12 about Moses.

_____

_____

_____

LESSONS LEARNED

⁎ Well-trained children can be used in great ways for the kingdom.

⁎ Miriam was doing as she had been instructed when an incidental, but hugely important, opportunity came her way. As we train our children to love God and walk in His ways, they can be powerful influences for good on their peers, on younger children, and on adults. More than a few souls have been led to Christ by children who, in their innocence, have pointed the way to Christ.

⁎ God's women should praise His deliverance. While the parting of the Red Sea was a divine feat rightfully summoning the praises of God's people, it pales when compared with His deliverance at Calvary from sin. Our praise should fill our prayers, our conversations, and our worship.

✳ The Lord is angered when we speak against His meek servants. We should apply this truth in the church today. Elders are ordained of God. Maligning their characters or undermining their authority is a personal affront to God Himself. First Timothy 5:19 contains a prohibition worthy of serious consideration.

✳ Often sin's penalty is partially paid by innocent people. A nation waited for seven days while Miriam observed the purification rite for one who was unclean. Canaan was calling, but the march toward the land of promise was suddenly interrupted. Thousands of people doing mundane daily tasks were changing their traveling plans, rearranging their schedules of activity, and making provisions for the extended encampment. No doubt it was discouraging for the women who had followed Miriam in exultant praise only a short time ago, to now be waiting on her pride as God's mission was delayed. Contrary to popular opinion, my sin is not always exclusively my business.

What are some specific sins of today that almost always exact penalties from innocent people?

_____

_____

_____

⪻ *Cindy's Reflections* ⪼

A Meek and Quiet Spirit

A meek and quiet spirit
Let me wear with joy, I pray.
Let those jewels of the heart
Grace my spirit, Lord, today.

Take from me the pearls of riches
That would keep me, Lord, from Thee.
Drape me with the pearls of wisdom
That Thy spirit I may see.

Let me not, like James and John,
Seek the place of grandest fame.
Remind me that the savior
As a servant humbly came.

Let me be the virtuous woman;
Seeking good through all my days.
Give me wealth far more than rubies;
In the gates, rewards of praise.

CHAPTER 4

PRINCESS OF PROVIDENCE

PHARAOH'S DAUGHTER

Discovery by the Princess

She was accustomed to riches the likes of which most of us could never fathom. She was the daughter of a Pharaoh. Her home was the palace, the "great house." The word *pharaoh* literally means "great house" and referred originally to the vast and lavish palace in which the Pharaohs lived. Egyptians believed that their Pharaohs were both gods and sons of gods. In theory, the people and lands of Egypt belonged to the Pharaoh. This power and wealth was seated in the home of the princess. She could beckon servants and, as we shall see, she seemed to get her way with the Pharaoh as well.

> ***Note to teacher:*** Have someone research ancient Egypt and bring to class a short report on life in the palace of the princess.

The baby Moses was floating in the flags of the Nile. Perhaps his mother had consciously placed him in the river's edge near a well-worn path. Perhaps many Egyptians passed daily along the river's edge as they walked to favorite bathing waters. This seems plausible from Exodus 2:3. "But when she could no longer hide him, she took an ark of bulrushes for him, daubed it with asphalt and pitch, put the child in it, and laid it in the reeds by the river's bank."

It seems that Miriam was expecting Moses to be found. The events that she was about to witness were phenomenal and central to the unfolding of God's vast plan for the redemption of mankind. The princess was about to become a tool in the hand of a Workman whose precision and purpose cannot be thwarted. She was about to become a piece in the puzzle of propitiation. She, in fact, was about to bring home the baby who would eventually bring down the kingdom!

Notice all of the details of the day that had to fall perfectly into place to secure a position in the palace for the baby Moses:

✳ Moses was in the right spot.

✳ The princess saw the basket.

✳ The princess decided to look in the basket.

✳ The baby wept.

❊ The princess had compassion.

❊ Miriam thought to offer Jochebed as a nurse.

❊ The princess decided to protect Moses from death.

So Moses was raised in the palace acquiring tools he would use one day to conquer it.

The little basket was really a mighty battleship. The baby, its captain, would be a mighty warrior of God. The little voice that was crying now would one day be the voice through which the Almighty would speak.

Moses was raised in the palace acquring tools he would use one day to conquer it.

Was the weather just right that day for bathing? Was it an accident that the maidens of the princess walked so near the river's edge as to spot the little ark? Was it an accident that the baby wept at just the right time to touch the tender heart of the young princess or was he pinched by an angel? Could Miriam's wisdom at this pivotal moment have been typical of a young girl her age? Would any other Egyptian who found a Hebrew baby boy have been allowed to keep it?

The point is obvious. No miracle occurred on this sunny day on the banks of the Nile. But God's hand was as surely protecting and providing on this day as it was on the day when the Red Sea parted.

FINDING GOD IN THE ORDINARY

Our God still protects and provides. He is as powerful in masterminding the ordinary—taking the myriad of natural occurrences and orchestrating them for His purposes—as He has ever been in His miraculous displays. Let us remember that, although the God we serve has chosen to place us in a non-miraculous era (1 Corinthians 13:8–10), He is still involved in the detailed workings of our world, and His power is infinite in that involvement. If we are about achieving the purposes of God, that providence and protection will become a staple of our spiritual security. "And we know that all things work together for good to those who love God, to those who are the called according to His purpose" (Romans 8:28).

Although this writer is certainly not qualified to expound on the process of the providence of Almighty God, I believe there are certain points about His natural intervention that are helpful to the Christian who struggles with finding God in the ordinary. Notice a few of them:

- Providence is not a biblical term but it is a biblical concept. The word *providence* does not appear in most translations of the New Testament. It does appear once in the King James Version in Acts 24:2. It refers there, not to any provision of God, but to that of a governor named Felix. But the truth that God does provide for His children is abundantly taught in many passages.

- Providence is not always material in nature. While there are passages that teach that God will provide the necessities of life for those who seek His kingdom first (Matthew 6:33), the additional blessings of good health and material prosperity may not always be in the best ultimate interests of God's children and their faith. Remember, God sees the whole picture of my life. He knows the strengths that often come with adversity and He knows the brevity of this life in comparison to eternity. His goal for me is heaven. If I begin to become discouraged with the provisions of my Father, let me remember Paul. As I read 2 Corinthians 11, let me be assured that God is in control of my life, even in the dark times. My God always has a plan.

Note the perils of Paul (2 Corinthians 11). What makes you believe that Paul was in God's realm of providence during these dark times?

____

____

- Providence, in our age, is never miraculous. The New Testament is clear in its teaching that miraculous gifts were only imparted through the laying on of the apostles' hands. Acts 8:14–18 is an excellent example of how the apostles were the only ones who could pass along this miracle-working power, and that such gifts were for the specific purpose of confirming the teachings of the apostles. Once the Holy Scriptures were complete, there was no need for that confirmation. Thus, today we have "that which is perfect" (1 Corinthians 13:8–10): the complete, inerrant Word of God. It doesn't take a miracle for us to know the will or power of God. We have all of that great wisdom and power in the book we call the Bible.

List additional Scriptures which prove that the age of miracles has ceased.

_____

_____

❊ Providence is best seen in retrospect. It's futile and dangerous to walk through my days in this life trying to figure out just how God is working in the everyday occurrences of my life. Let me illustrate. I may believe God opens a career opportunity because He wants me to spend my life in a certain field of work. But His purpose may be bigger. He may be introducing me to my life's mate or bringing me into contact with someone I may convert to be a great leader in His church. He may be simply using this career opportunity as a stepping stone to another opportunity that is suited for His purposes. It's great to look back and see how God has used certain events or trials for His glory in my life. It's great to trust and anticipate with assurance that He will make the puzzle beautiful as He assembles all the pieces of my life. But to attempt to interpret the events of my life through the eyes of God at the time they are occurring is futile. I cannot know the intended outcomes. He can. If I jump to conclusions about why He is working in a certain way in my life, then I may run ahead of Him and pursue courses that are contrary to His will.

❋ Providence is a prayer partner. God hears and answers my prayers. The fact that prayers today are answered is clearly a biblical truth. Yet God does not supernaturally or miraculously reach in and alter the eventualities that occur around us. Thus, the means by which He answers prayers today must be natural means. I should be sure that my prayers are fervent, and that my petitions are unselfish. I should work to mold my will to His and express my willful conformity to His purposes for me (Matthew 26:39). Then I should trust that He is answering my prayers with the pity that a father has for his children (Psalm 103:13). Remember, a good father doesn't give his son everything for which he asks. Let me illustrate. A good father knows that the painful needle injected into the child's skin contains the antibiotic that will cure the deadly disease. The child cries with anguish when the doctor gives the shot. Does the father heed the child's cries and stop the painful process? No. The father insists upon the administration of the treatment, because he's the father. In this case, he knows the outcome. His very refusal to grant the child's petition is a father's providence. He is providing, through the painful experience, what is best for the child.

Look retrospectively for God's providence that has worked to bring glory to God through your life. Write your experience below:

_____

_____

_____

❋ Providence is amazing! To me it seems incredible—more than any miracle—that my God can take millions of circumstances that prevail in the lives of His children and make them work together for the ultimate benefit of those children and for the accomplishment of His purposes in our world.

If God can make the arms of the daughter of the throne cradle the Israelite leader, the leader who would later bring that throne to its knees, God can make my life a channel of His power. If God can, in one day, so reverse circumstances as to make a threatened slave baby an honored prince in the palace, so can He orchestrate my life to achieve His purposes in His divine kingdom. He is able!

> *Note to teacher:* Find the hymn written by L. O. Sanderson called "The Providence of God" and share its lyrics with the class. Have the class sing it together.

WHO SAVED THE BABY?

Did a Hebrew midwife save the baby? Did Jochebed save the baby? Did the little boat save the baby? Did the water that floated the little boat save the baby? Did the princess save the baby? Did Pharaoh save the baby at his daughter's request? Did God save the baby? All of these people and things saved the baby. God orchestrated them all.

WHO SAVES US?

Does faith save us? Does grace save us? Does obedience save us? Does water save us? Does God save us? Does the Word save us? Does the blood save us? Does preaching save us? Does Jesus save us? If I say I am saved by grace, does that mean I am not saved by faith? Of course not (Ephesians 2:5). If I say I am saved by baptism (1 Peter 3:21), does that mean I am not saved by the blood? No. My soul contacts the saving blood in baptism (Romans 6:3). If I say I am saved by preaching, does that mean I am not saved by the gospel? No, for it is Christ crucified that is preached (1 Corinthians 1:21–23). All of these things save us. It is God who orchestrates them all. That is why we call it God's plan of salvation.

God can orchestrate my life to acheive His purposes. He is able!

List all of the things from Scripture that save men; give a Scripture for each item listed.

HEAR: Jn 6:45; Acts 2:22   BELIEVE: Acts 2:22
REPENT: Acts 2:38   CONFESS: Rom 10:9-10
BAPTIZE: Acts 2:38

⇒ Cindy's Reflections ⇐

My Place in His World

When the crimson leaves have fallen
And cool winds breathe a sigh,
I stop beneath a barren oak
And wistfully think, "Why?"

Why must flowers lose their blooms?
Where goes the butterfly?
And why does autumn bear a chill?
Where do the birds go and why?

The squirrels don't forget to find acorns.
The fields never fail to turn gold.
The mice find my barn for the winter;
And I've turned another year old.

Every appointment of nature
Is met with the greatest detail.
How can all heav'n and earth do His will
And I, in His own image fail?

If I could, like stars in their courses,
Or that gold harvest moon in the night,
Follow the course He has charted
And change when He thought it was right;

If I had no fear of tomorrow;
If I trusted in God's wisdom more;
Like the squirrel I'd be ready for winter
Like the bird flying south, I could soar.

The heavens and earth shout His glory,
The sky is the work of His hand.
I have a place in my God's world.
I, too, must attend His command.

Seedtime and harvest, death before life
In His time, may I take my place.
As the whole world gives way and all nature obeys,
In the seasons may I see His face.

CHAPTER 5

MARRIED TO THE MIRACLE MAN

ZIPPORAH

A BIG CHANGE

Zipporah, like most of us, lived her life in relative anonymity. Though she was married to Moses, the greatest man of God and arguably the greatest societal leader of his day, she is one of the Bible's less distinguished women. There is really only one incident recorded in which Zipporah reveals something of her character. It is with this occasion in Exodus 4:18–26 that we will give attention in this lesson.

Moses had met Zipporah, one of seven daughters of the priest of Midian, in the wilderness of Midian. Like Rachel and Rebekah, her first connection with Israel was at a well. It seems that she and her sisters had gone to draw water for the flocks. Exodus 2:16–17 reveals that they were in the middle of the watering task when a group of shepherds interrupted their work, pushing them aside. These shepherds likely used their brawn to intimidate the sisters into relinquishing the water supply. What the shepherds didn't know was that they were actually up against an experienced intercessor. Moses had fought for the underdog before and he did not have a sympathetic eye for the bully (Exodus 2:11–15). So Moses stood up for the maidens, was invited to dinner at the house of the priest, and subsequently was given Zipporah as a wedding gift—a gift so there would be a wedding!

Zipporah had been the daughter of a shepherd. Now she was the wife of a shepherd. Sometimes marriage leads us down a comfortable and familiar path. This was likely the case as Zipporah settled into married life, remaining with her father's nomadic clan in Midian. But a burning bush was about to change all of that!

One day Moses came in from work and told Zipporah that they would be moving. They were not just moving to another spot on the farm, but Moses went on to say they were moving to Egypt. They were not going back to the palace where Moses' foster family lived, either. They were going to join voluntarily a nation of slaves who were under a mighty oppression. In fact, Moses revealed to Zipporah that he, personally, was taking on the job of deliverer for this nation.

Now Zipporah had likely grown up in an idolatrous family. We must give her credit for following this man of Jehovah God to do the great mission for which he had been called at the burning bush. She must have developed quite a faith in Jehovah, for the incredible story Moses told her of the burning bush put her on a donkey with her two boys headed for the greatest empire on earth. From a front row seat she was about to witness a miraculous deliverance. If she needed more faith, she was about to receive a divine supplement!

> What do you think was involved in Zipporah's making the adjustment from shepherd's wife to wife of the mighty deliverer?
>
> _____
>
> _____
>
> _____
>
> What indicates her submissiveness to Moses' leadership?
>
> *She apparently volutarily followed Moses into a very different life*

A BIG CHALLENGE

Exodus 4:24 is an amazing and perplexing passage. Moses was God's chosen deliverer. He was later to be described as the meekest man in the earth and one who was faithful in the house of God (Numbers 12:3–7 KJV). Yet in this passage, God was seeking to kill him. I believe God was showing extreme displeasure that Moses had ignored His command to circumcise his son, likely the youngest son, Eliezer.

> Zipporah was married to the meekest man in all the earth (Numbers 12:3 KJV). Define *meekness.*
>
> *patient, mild, Gentle*
>
> _____
>
> _____
>
> What blessings would a meek man bring into the marriage relationship?
>
> _____
>
> _____
>
> _____

Circumcision was the fleshly mark of Hebrew males. Although it was not exclusively a Hebrew rite (the Egyptians practiced it in ancient times), it contained special significance for Israel because it was a spiritual seal of the Abrahamic covenant (Genesis 17:14–21). It was performed on the eighth day after birth (Leviticus 12:3). If strangers were admitted to the Jewish commonwealth, they too were required to be circumcised. God was serious—dead serious in this case—about the significance of circumcision. How could Moses ever be the undisputed leader and deliverer of the circumcised nation when his family had not completely complied with this fleshly marking of the covenant?

Moses was clearly the object of the wrath of God.

So the little family stopped at an inn on the way to Egypt, surely expecting a good night's sleep before the continuation of a long and tedious passageway to the execution of a monumental feat of deliverance. Surely they were all aware that God's presence, yea His divine assurance and intervention, was absolutely essential if Moses was to stand before this monarch with any confidence. Yet God was about to make it clear that complete compliance was necessary to maintain the covenant relationship that was Moses' source of confidence.

The inn was not peaceful. Moses was being stalked by a would-be killer. But in this case, the stalker was omnipotent and omniscient. He had no trouble finding Moses or revealing His contempt for Moses' failure to circumcise his son.

Moses was clearly the object of the wrath of God. It seems that Zipporah knew that her husband was in deep trouble. She evidently knew the reason for God's displeasure. So she seemingly took matters into her own hands, did the required surgery, and threw the foreskin at Moses' feet as if to symbolically place the blame for the family's distress at the feet of her husband, Moses.

Many scholars believe Zipporah's behavior in the inn was shamefully rebellious and needlessly violent. While this view is widely accepted, the evidence seems overwhelming that her behavior was a reasoned response to Moses' failure to obey God's express command of circumcision. After all, she was aware that the practice was required, for she had given birth to two sons, one of whom had been circumcised. Her husband was a circumcised

Hebrew. Her father later expressed a clear belief in Jehovah (Exodus 18:1–12). It seems unlikely that Zipporah's actions were motivated by uncontrolled anger. It makes more sense to notice that she had a motive both to circumcise her son and to be frustrated with the spiritual ineptitude of her family leader, one who, ironically, had just been tapped to lead a huge nation from bondage. It seems obvious that she saw a need for consistency in Moses' personal life before he attempted this huge and very public deliverance. One could even go so far as to surmise that Zipporah deflected the anger of the Almighty toward Moses.

CIRCUMCISION TODAY

While the law of Moses was replete with rituals and outward displays of devotion—read the book of Leviticus and you cannot overlook this emphasis—the New Covenant does not emphasize ordinances and physical rituals, but a spiritual kingdom and a symbolic circumcision of the heart. Colossians 2:11–13 suggests that baptism, the point at which sins are put off, is the spiritual circumcision of God's people today. Notice this passage:

> In Him you were also circumcised with the circumcision made without hands, by putting off the body of the sins of the flesh, by the circumcision of Christ, buried with Him in baptism, in which you also were raised with Him through faith in the working of God, who raised Him from the dead. And you, being dead in your trespasses and the uncircumcision of your flesh, He has made alive together with Him, having forgiven you all trespasses (Colossians 2:11–13).

Baptism is God's surgical removal of sin. We are spiritual Jews today, God's chosen people, only if we have circumcised hearts.

> For he is not a Jew who is one outwardly, nor is circumcision that which is outward in the flesh; but he is a Jew who is one inwardly; and circumcision is that of the heart, in the Spirit, not in the letter; whose praise is not from men but from God (Romans 2:28–29).

How important was circumcision to God?

_____

_____

Find New Testament passages that underscore the importance of the circumcision of the heart today.

_____

_____

LIFE WITH A GREAT LEADER

Zipporah. She was just a wilderness shepherdess who came upon a man one day: a man who would see a talking burning bush; a man who, with the rod of God, would turn a river into blood and part a mighty sea. Zipporah's life was never to be routine or boring again. She was to learn from a personal vantage point the power of the Almighty and the blessings of being a part of his circumcised Israel.

In this lesson, God sought to kill Moses. Find his conversation with God later in Numbers 11 that includes his petition of discouragement—asking God to let him die. Why isn't it easy to be married to leaders who are subject to discouragement and criticism?

_____

_____

_____

Suggest ways that elders' and preachers' wives can bolster and encourage godly husbands during discouraging times.

_____

_____

Suggest ways leaders' wives can deal with their own pressures (for example: time sacrifices, very high expectations from others, and added emotional burdens).

_____

_____

Cindy's Reflections

Home

It can be a place of refuge
For the burdened and oppressed;
For His weary, wand'ring soldier
It can be a place of rest.

An institute of higher learning . . .
A school in living from life's start;
For the highest form of learning
Is the training of the heart.

And within its walls, a mission
For the guilty, sin-sick soul;
A lighthouse for the rescue
Of a life that's lost control.

It's a bustling place of business
For the Father up above;
But for those who dwell within
A peaceful haven of His love.

It's a garden for the sowing;
Tender hearts, its fertile ground
And its blossoms spring eternal
In the soul that's glory bound!

CHAPTER 6

WOMAN WITH AN AUDIENCE

COZBI

Cozbi's name means deceitful. Her story is one of sexual shame and idolatry. More importantly, her story graphically illustrates the disdain of God toward blatant sin in His camp. Ironically, God used the shameless Cozbi to establish His covenant of peace with one who was unashamed to stand for right. She reminds God's people today to be serious about the sanctification to which God calls us. We are to come out from among them and be separate (2 Corinthians 6:17).

Setting the Stage

The saga of Cozbi occurs during the last year of Israel's wilderness wanderings. The magnificent promises of the land of corn and wine are on their immediate horizon. The generation that trembled in fear at the inhabitants of Canaan (Numbers 13–14) has now been replaced by a generation that seems not only fearless, but fraternizing with the riotous people of Canaan. Balaam, a Midianite seer, but one through whom Jehovah spoke to the Midianites, had desired and pleaded with God for permission to prophesy against Israel and favorably toward his sister nation Moab. God's anger had been kindled against Balaam (Numbers 22:22) because he went with the princes of Moab to meet with their king, who had courted his favor by promising him great honor if he would only curse Israel. God had powerfully shown through a talking donkey that Balaam's proposed alliance with Moab against Israel was potentially destructive for him and the lands of Moab and Midian (Numbers 22:22–35).

But Israel should have heard the donkey's message, too. In Numbers 25:1–3, we see that while God was blessing Israel and cursing her enemies, Israel herself was busy making sinful alliances with the very nations God was cursing.

> Now Israel remained in Acacia Grove, and the people began to commit harlotry with the women of Moab. They invited the people to the sacrifices of their gods, and the people ate and bowed down to their gods. So Israel was joined to Baal of Peor, and the anger of the Lord was aroused against Israel (Numbers 25:1–3).

Notice the three progressive steps Israel took to wholesale idolatry.

First, the men of Israel began to commit whoredom with the daughters of Moab. Even casual observation by anyone who does counseling shows that sexual sin binds with cords stronger than any other sin. (Read Proverbs 5 and note particularly verse 22.) Men are often willing to forfeit their jobs, homes, children, relationships with parents, and fellowship with godly people in order to continue illicit sexual relationships. Fornication and adultery have even caused men to verbally admit that they are willing to be lost in hell eternally in order to continue in this sin. As one man I know put it, "If my relationship with her is going to keep me out of heaven, I'd rather have my heaven now." I wonder if this person believes he will schedule his own personal itinerary for hell, as well.

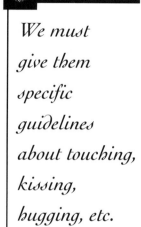

We must give them specific guidelines about touching, kissing, hugging, etc.

Second, the people became involved in the idolatry of Moab. "They invited the people to the sacrifices of their gods, and the people ate and bowed down to their gods" (Numbers 25:2).

Sexual involvement with ungodly partners is sinful and shameful within itself. But the spiritual ruin that it leaves in its wake for entire families is devastating. Young people in our congregations need to hear strong teaching from early ages about sexual purity before marriage. Older women need to be in classrooms teaching young girls specifics about purity of heart, discretion in dating behavior, and the choosing of godly companions. Most importantly, mothers need to accept the burden of responsibility in molding the young hearts within their care to reject Satan's mentality of sexual freedom. This mentality has so weakened America's moral climate, her political strength, and her health—notice these three weaknesses were obvious in Israel in Numbers 25—that her very foundation is shaken. Raising children who will not be pulled away from God via sexual sin in such a society is indeed a formidable challenge. It will take more than general cautionary statements about purity when our children become teens. We must, from very young ages, instruct and require compliance regarding modesty in dress and separation from the world in entertainment choices. We must give them specific guidelines about touching, kissing, hugging, and general propriety in relationships with members of the opposite sex. This takes a great deal of fortitude and large quantities of time spent with our children. I heard about a mom in my neighborhood who, upon hearing that her young daughter had a boyfriend in the house each afternoon for a couple of hours, responded by saying, "Okay, that does it! She goes on birth control tomorrow! How I would love to come home right now and catch her with him, but I have a hair appointment." No wonder her daughter had no sense of moral values! The best form of birth control is parent control, and it is dispensed far in advance of the teen years.

The devil is very busy getting his propaganda about safe sex to your children. He uses school courses, organizations like Planned Parenthood, and centers for disease control. He leans heavily on mass media: television, movies, CDs, and the Internet. He does it most powerfully through peers. It will not be an accident if my children enter God-approved marriages in purity. It will be a product of several factors, including prayer, instruction, time, discipline, and Bible study.

Search for current statistics about promiscuity in America to bring to class. Are trends leaning more toward God's standard of purity or progressively moving toward blatant sexual immorality?

_____

_____

_____

What are some things parents can do, while their children are preteens, to help them to determine to date only godly young people?

_____

_____

_____

Once sexually involved with Moab, the Israelites were only a short step away from idolatry. Though twenty-first century idols in America are not statues of stone or carvings of wood, they nonetheless pull allegiance from Jehovah, giving it to whatever the godless society worships. The gods of today are most often materialism (Colossians 3:5), sexual pleasure (Romans 1:23–24), and entertainment (2 Timothy 3:4).

It is interesting to note that it was contextually the men in verse 1 who were committing whoredom. But it was the people in verse 2 who were bowing to the gods of the Moabites. Sin grows proportionally in severity and scope. When fathers fall to Satan, their families are often close behind.

Consider television and its portrayal of various perversions. Consider also the introduction of homosexual leaders in various religious groups. Give other examples in current American culture of the flaunting of sexual sin.

_____

_____

_____

Third, Israel was joined to Baal-Peor. "So Israel was joined to Baal of Peor, and the anger of the Lord was aroused against Israel" (Numbers 25:3). Satan seeks solidarity among his allies. Becoming friendly with his forces puts one in the danger zone that borders the full scale Baal alliance. God's response to this joining was extreme anger.

What is the meaning of the word Baal?

fertility God

_____

_____

The anger of the Lord was aroused against Israel. Then the Lord said to Moses, "Take all the leaders of the people and hang the offenders before the Lord, out in the sun, that the fierce anger of the Lord may turn away from Israel." So Moses said to the judges of Israel, "Every one of you kill his men who were joined to Baal of Peor" (Numbers 25:3–5).

Let no one doubt that God is a jealous God (Deuteronomy 5:9). Let no one doubt His wrath (Romans 1:18).

Let all know that He is a consuming fire (Hebrews 12:29). Twenty-four thousand lives were required before Cozbi came on the scene, and through a series of events the plague was stayed.

God doesn't send death plagues today to punish sin. This does not mean He is no longer a God of wrath! Find a passage that shows He is reserving or saving up His wrath for those who are rebellious toward Him.

_____

_____

_____

Explain why it is important that our children marry Christians.

_____

_____

_____

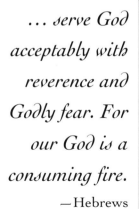

... serve God acceptably with reverence and Godly fear. For our God is a consuming fire.

—Hebrews 12:28–29

ENTER COZBI

Families were weeping as they witnessed the hanging deaths of loved ones. This method of execution was not left to human discretion. There were no appellate courts to prolong life for the guilty. God was prosecutor, judge, and jury. Twenty-four thousand were already dead. Millions were in mourning.

In this setting Cozbi enters the camp. Her appearance was a blatant and blasphemous slap in the face of God. While weeping multitudes were being humbled by the death plague, Zimri, an influential Simeonite, brought his adulteress publicly and pridefully before his brethren. In the somber setting of God's wrath being dispensed, he displayed this whoredom before the assembly that now wept as a result of the consequences of such whoredom. Furthermore, Cozbi wasn't just any old Midianite maiden. She was a princess of Midian. Zimri's alliance was not only with an immoral woman of Midian. His alliance was with the influential and important idolaters (Numbers 25:15).

THE FINAL ACT

Phinehas, the grandson of Aaron, was incensed by the utter defiance of Zimri. He followed Zimri to the pavilion and graphically illustrated for all of Israel God's disdain for his arrogance. "And he went after the man of Israel into the tent and thrust both of them through, the man of Israel, and the woman through her body. So the plague was stopped among the children of Israel" (Numbers 25:8).

God was pleased with the zeal of Phinehas. He established with Phinehas His covenant of peace. When blatant sin is in the camp today, God expects His people to address it and purify His congregation (1 Corinthians 5). The plague was stayed and the healing process was begun. God reordered the smiting of the Midianites and reissued His warnings about the beguiling nature of the idolatrous peoples of Canaan. He was preparing their hearts for the challenges that lay ahead, for they were about to enter Canaan, a land they were to rid of idolatrous multitudes. How could Israel fail to recognize at this point the oneness of Jehovah and His wrath on those who would divide their allegiance?

God's covenant of peace was given to Phinehas after the slaying of Zimri and Cozbi when His justice was met. How do sinful people today meet the requirements of God's justice?

_____

_____

_____

How do people today enter His covenant of peace?

_____

_____

_____

THE CURTAIN CLOSES (LESSONS LEARNED)

✳ Joining the devil's forces is a progressive decline rather than a sudden fall.

✳ Sexual sin binds with strong cords.

✳ It is a fearful thing to fall into the hands of the living God (Hebrews 10:31).

✳ Blatant and intentional sin must be biblically confronted by people of God.

Cindy's Reflections

Whatever!

Whatever is honest . . . Whatever is true;
Whatever I'm thinking controls what I do.
Whatever is just . . . Whatever is pure . . .
Whatever my sin, heal my heart for its cure.
Whatever is lovely and good, Lord I pray,
Get into my heart. From its throne guide my way.
If my heart can find virtue, O God, let me live it.
If someone is worthy of praise, let me give it.
Wherever the bend in my pathway may lead;
Whatever the struggle, whatever the need;
Whatever my heart . . . when it suffers or sings;
Whatever! O Lord, may I think on these things.

Finally, brethren, whatsoever things *are* true,
whatsoever things *are* honest,
whatsoever things *are* just,
whatsoever things *are* pure,
whatsoever things *are* lovely,
whatsoever things *are* of good report;
if there be any virtue, and if *there be* any praise,
think on these things.

—Philippians 4:8 KJV

CHAPTER 7

ASK!
THE DAUGHTERS OF ZELOPHEHAD

NO BROTHERS

Mahlah, Noah, Hoglah, Milcah, and Tirzah. I've never heard a sermon an on any of these women. None of my friends have named their little girls after any of them. But their inclusion in this study is not the pursuit of trivia. It is rather the pursuit of truth that God has revealed by their inclusion in Scripture.

The first reference to these women is found in Numbers 26:33: "Now Zelophehad the son of Hepher had no sons, but daughters; and the names of the daughters of Zelophehad were Mahlah, Noah, Hoglah, Milcah, and Tirzah."

Here they are simply mentioned in a census taken just prior to the Israelites' entry into Canaan. We find here that they are of the tribe of Manasseh and that they have no brothers. Since family land parcels were dispensed through male heirs, the indication is that the family of Zelophehad would receive no land in Canaan.

BUT THEY ASKED . . .

WITH INITIATIVE

Numbers 27 opens with the courage and initiative of these five unmarried women motivating them to approach the door of the tabernacle to speak with Moses, Eleazar, and all the princes to make a petition for land. The distribution of land was an important part of God's plan for Israel for several obvious reasons. First, it was an efficient economic system to retain all land within the original family to whom it was distributed. This system helped to maintain a degree of social equality throughout God's nation. More importantly, it preserved a meticulously organized registry through which the Judaic lineage of the Messiah could one day be traced. By passing the distributed land to the sons, the inheritance stayed within the family of original ownership.

But no one had ever asked if an exception to this inheritance law could be made in a case in which there were no sons. This was the significant plea of these five sisters:

> Our father died in the wilderness; but he was not in the company of those who gathered together against the Lord, in company with Korah, but he died in his own sin; and he had no sons. Why should the name of our father be removed from among his family because he had no son? Give us a possession among our father's brothers (Numbers 27:3–4).

Pause for a moment to think about this desire-turned-plea, later to turn blessing. Do you think God knew of the plight of the daughters of Zelophehad prior to their request through Moses? Was he already cognizant that these five women legally had no claim to a home place in Canaan?

Of course he knew. He knew how many hairs were on each of their heads (Matthew 10:30). He knew when they sat down and when they stood (Psalm 139:2a). He even knew that they were wishing for an inheritance before they themselves knew (Psalm 139:2b). God knows our needs, our desires, and our pleas long before we turn them into prayers. But He wants us to turn our longings heavenward. Just as I want to hear my children express their dependence on me, so God the Father wants to hear us express our needs and wishes. How many blessings are reserved in your name just waiting to be claimed by the asking? Ask!

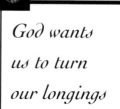

God wants us to turn our longings heavenward. Ask!

Luke 11:5–13 contains a powerful lesson about persistence in prayer. God wants us to prove our faith and fervency by bringing our petitions often. Consistency and persistency in prayer display the initiative and sense of dependency God wants us to have in our communication with Him.

Why do you think the woman's request was granted in Luke 11:5–13?

_____

_____

_____

What characteristic did she portray that is also a necessary ingredient for a faithful prayer?

_____

WITH MEEKNESS

It is interesting to think of all the ways these girls could have handled this dilemma. They could have risen up in bitterness against God's system and against His leader, Moses, as Miriam did on one occasion (Numbers 12). They could have resorted to sinful incest in order to preserve a male heir as did the daughters of Lot (Genesis 19:32). They could have caused a mighty uproar by rallying others behind their cause as did Korah, Dathan, and Abiram in Numbers 16. But it wasn't in their blood (Numbers 27:3).

Imagine five women in modern day America being denied an inheritance on the basis of gender. Based on current standards, we would expect them to react with deep insult. Then we would expect to hear a lot of rhetoric about equal rights. Feminist leaders would delight in CNN coverage of interviews with these five heroines of their cause. We would certainly expect a civil suit. But they simply and meekly petitioned God through Moses, God's chosen intercessor.

Surely much of faithfulness in the life of a Christian woman today pertains not merely to how she acts, but to how she reacts. This is especially true when she perceives that some injustice has been directed toward her. While we would never endorse legal injustice, meekly and respectfully seeking equitable solutions through proper channels displays the spirit of godly women. The "I am woman, hear me roar" mentality is not becoming to women of God.

> Share an example of a woman's seeking to use proper channels to resolve an injustice suffered in the church.
>
> _____
>
> _____
>
> _____

WITH FAITH

The intercessor today is Christ. The avenue of prayer is perhaps our most neglected resource as Christian women. So often we tend to exhaust every available possibility of resolve to our conflicts before we lay them at His throne. Jesus said, "Ask, and it will be given to you." We're admonished by inspiration in 1 Peter 5:7 to cast our cares upon Him, for He cares for us. This verse literally means that He will do the caring *for* us or in our stead. When we have unresolved issues in our lives, particularly those that involve our spiritual inheritance, our first resources should be prayer and Bible study: asking and seeking.

James 1:5 has provided a staple in my daily prayer petitions for many years. It reads: "If any of you lacks wisdom, let him ask of God, who gives to all liberally and without reproach, and it will be given to him."

I don't do mornings without this plea for wisdom. No mother should. I love the details of its wonderful providence of wisdom.

I love the word *any*. It's all-inclusive. It means me.

I love the word *ask*. It carries no huge requirements of prestige or riches. It's something that even I can do.

I love the word *God*. This is not wisdom of Dr. Brazelton, Dr. Phil, or Dr. Laura, or even my minister. This is heavenly wisdom.

I love the word *liberally*. God will not give me a trifling little handful of wisdom. It's a heaping helping of heavenly wisdom.

I love the word *will*. It's such an unconditional little word. There is no ambiguity here. It's not that I might be given wisdom. It's a sure thing. I don't do mornings without this prayer.

I heard recently through my friend Melony about a woman who lives in the hills of East Tennessee. She prefers, for nostalgic reasons, to run her household without electricity and running water. Although her home is plumbed and wired for electricity, she cooks over a wood stove, draws water from a well, and warms by the wood hearth. She reads by the light of an oil lamp and sews by hand. She prefers to live without these conveniences although they are readily available. This lifestyle may be well and good when we're speaking of electricity and water. But as God's children today, we are connected to the greatest source of light, warmth, power, and living water available to mankind. Yet so often we just fail to turn on the lights. We fail to drink! We need to be women of prayer. A-S-K!

Write on a separate sheet of paper—and note below—three of God's prayer promises that have come to mean a great deal to you.

_____

_____

_____

Give your paper to the class teacher, who may wish to make each class member a bookmark or refrigerator magnet of prayer promises.

WHAT GOD ALTERED

It is important to notice that what God amended in the case of Zelophehad's daughters was a civil law, having to do with land distribution, rather than a spiritual or moral law. God's spiritual laws for Israel were unchanging, staying intact until all was fulfilled at Calvary (Hebrews 9). The new law or covenant that came into effect when Christ died, unlike the law of Moses, is a spiritual covenant, exclusive of civil or national law. In our dispensation, God has delegated civil authority to governments (Romans 13). Thus, the written New Testament law, under which we serve, is God's final, unchanging spiritual will, never to be altered. We should not petition God for changes in His spiritual requirements, but rather plead, as Christ instructed in the model prayer, for His will to be done (Matthew 6:10).

> *It is easy for us to come to believe that God's laws for man evolve as society changes.*

It is easy for us as Christians in a society of subjectivism to come to believe that God's laws for man evolve as society changes. For example, in the few days prior to this writing, over two thousand homosexual couples were married in San Francisco. The months prior to this writing have seen a major U.S. denomination divide because of the ordination of a homosexual priest in that particular religion. The written laws of God regarding this sin have not changed (1 Corinthians 6:9). It is difficult for us to accept His word as unchanging universal truth. Though His will can be altered by the prayers of His faithful children, His written laws are non-negotiable. His word abides forever (Psalm 119:160).

Write a Scripture reference that shows the universal or eternal nature of God's laws.

LONG-TERM EFFECTS OF THEIR PETITION

God, the perfectly just Judge, ruled in favor of the five brave daughters of Zelophehad. He granted them an inheritance, thus preserving the name of their father. The written law is recorded in Numbers 36:6–9:

> This is what the Lord commands concerning the daughters of Zelophehad, saying, "Let them marry whom they think best, but they may marry only within the family of their father's tribe." So the inheritance of the children of Israel shall not change hands from tribe to tribe, for every one of the children of Israel shall keep the inheritance of the tribe of his fathers. And every daughter who possesses an inheritance in any tribe of the children of Israel shall be the wife of one of the family of her father's tribe, so that the children of Israel each may possess the inheritance of his fathers. Thus no inheritance shall change hands from one tribe to another, but every tribe of the children of Israel shall keep its own inheritance.

God placed restrictions on the exception made for these women. They were required to marry men within their tribe. In this way, the inheritance would never move from tribe to tribe. They married sons of Manasseh who were actually their first cousins (Numbers 36:11–12).

Notice also that their plea produced a law for all future generations of Israelite women who found themselves in situations void of male heirs. Pleas to heaven can indeed have long-range effects.

Share an example of someone who was granted a prayer petition with long reaching effects—either in your lifetime or in Bible times. Such examples are encouraging to those who are currently persisting in fervent and righteous prayer.

_____

_____

_____

⇒ *Cindy's Reflections* ⇒

When My Cup Overflows

Red Kool-Aid on the carpet, Fruit Loops on the floor,
Magic marker on the wall, mud prints at the door;
The whining of a toddler, the mood swings of a teen,
The non-stop chatter about trivia of the one that's in-
        between.

The youngest won't let you out of sight: he eternally tugs
        at your blouse.
The oldest pretends not to know you at all; she'd rather
        you'd stay in the house.
The day in and day out of being a mom; the pains and
        misgivings of growing;
The messes and stresses are just evidence that my blessing
        cup's overflowing.

This house is too big. I can't keep it clean!
The dishwasher's been broken and now the washing
        machine!
I've got way too much e-mail . . . no time to reply,
I'll never do all this ironing so I won't even try.
I pick up the paper and read of a drought;
A whole country in Asia where food's running out.
Why did I complain? We've food to keep healthy,
A big house that's warm, good friends, we are wealthy!

Lord, help me remember, my Father's a King.
I'm an heir in Your kingdom! You own everything!
Stop me from murmuring, Lord. Let me look up
From blessings innumerable poured into my cup.

Let me see You, Father, in the riches you give.
May I multiply them each day that I live.
If I can give comfort instead of just seeking it,
If some word could help some soul just in my speaking it;

Help me to know it, Lord; help me to see
Each golden chance that You offer to me.
Fill up my cup, Lord, but each time I drink;
As I taste of Your mercies, O Lord, make me think

Someone is thirsty, Lord . . . someone my heart knows.
Show me that cup, Lord, when mine overflows.

CHAPTER 8

PEOPLE CAN CHANGE

RAHAB

SHE WAS A HARLOT . . .

> Now Joshua the son of Nun sent out two men from Acacia Grove to spy secretly, saying, "Go, view the land, especially Jericho." So they went, and came to the house of a harlot named Rahab, and lodged there (Joshua 2:1).

Some who have studied Rahab have attempted to sugar-coat the fact that Rahab was a prostitute. In reading her incredible story, I came across those who insisted that she wasn't really a harlot at all in the sense that we

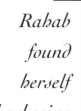

Rahab found herself harboring the enemy spies . . .

think of harlotry today. She is styled by such liberal theorists as merely a hospitable innkeeper or tavern maiden. Others admit her harlotry, but would have us to believe that harlotry was a respectable way to earn a living in Rahab's society. Neither of these theories finds any basis in Scripture, and certainly our imaginations would have to be stretched into areas of wild supposition to assume that Rahab's lifestyle prior to her encounter with the people of God was anything more noble than the demeaning portrait of prostitution with which we are all too familiar in our modern society.

Rahab's home business was built on the huge protective wall that surrounded Jericho. Historians tell us that there were likely two walls surrounding Jericho. There was a space of twelve to fifteen feet between the two walls. Rahab's house was probably situated above these two walls or foundationally supported by the walls themselves and by the cross beams laid between them.

Archeologists believe Jericho to be one of the world's oldest cities, and certainly it was one of the best fortified ancient cities. Lying in the fertile plain between the Jordan River and the Mediterranean Sea, its mild climate and well-watered vicinity made it attractive to invaders. Its huge and likely doubled walls were made of massive stones, each probably about thirty feet long, eight feet wide, and three-and-a-half feet high. The walls made the city unattractive to enemy armies, that is, unless an army could just walk around the city and blow on rams' horns, at which time the walls would collapse.

A portion of this gargantuan wall was probably one of the walls of Rahab's house or, as described above, the foundation of her house. She could, from the vantage point of her roof, see both the town of Jericho and the plain outside the fortress. This situation was likely a plus in the business of prostitution, for it provided Rahab with knowledge of the comings and goings of the men of the city and of the strangers as they made their way to Jericho.

SHE HARBORED . . .

Perhaps it was the strategic location of Rahab's house on the wall of Jericho that brought the spies into her house. God had not yet told Joshua just how the walls were to be breached. An inspection of the walls would certainly have been a reasonable use of their time in the city. We must assume that their actions were honorable during their stay in Jericho. They were there, after all, at the command of Joshua, God's chosen leader, and they reported directly back to him all that had occurred during the mission (Joshua 2:23).

So Rahab found herself harboring the enemy spies, the very men who planned to take all the defensive secrets of Jericho back to Israel, only to return shortly for the capture and destruction of her home town.

SHE HEARD . . .

Faith comes by hearing (Romans 10:17), and it was a great faith planted in the heart of Rahab upon her hearing of the mighty works of the Lord in behalf of His Israel.

I wish that all who hear of the mighty deliverance of Jehovah today would respond with the same honesty and humility that characterized Rahab. Whatever she was before her encounter with the people of God is not nearly as significant as the heart of humble submission she manifested when she was given a window of opportunity to demonstrate faith in Jehovah. Would that my heart and yours melt in awe of His judgments! Would that our human courage surrender in reverent fear for the "God in heaven above and in the earth beneath"!

For all of us in America today, there remains no excuse. We have all "heard these things." We know the story of the manger, the cross, and the greatest deliverance of all at the empty tomb. We know about the mighty ruler, the prince of darkness (John 12:31), who has been conquered by our

Lord. But so many today are willing to continue to rely on man-made walls of defense, willing to continue to dwell upon some man-made fortress of doctrine or human ingenuity rather than to allow their hearts to melt and seek out His way of deliverance. They fail to see that no wall erected by man is large enough to protect us from impending destruction when God decides that the wall will crumble. How defenseless are those who continue to dwell on the wall!

SHE HID . . .

Rahab hid the spies.

> So the king of Jericho sent to Rahab, saying, "Bring out the men who have come to you, who have entered your house, for they have come to search out all the country." Then the woman took the two men and hid them. So she said, "Yes, the men came to me, but I did not know where they were from. And it happened as the gate was being shut, when it was dark, that the men went out. Where the men went I do not know; pursue them quickly, for you may overtake them." (But she had brought them up to the roof and hidden them with the stalks of flax, which she had laid in order on the roof.) Then the men pursued them by the road to the Jordan, to the fords. And as soon as those who pursued them had gone out, they shut the gate (Joshua 2:3–7).

Rahab's display of faith was not limited to a mere confession of belief in the God of Israel. She courageously stepped outside the box, and acted upon her belief in Jehovah, even though it put her at odds with, and in danger of, the culture around her. She put it all on the line when the king's men knocked at her door. She had an immediate decision to make. Was her trust in the powers of the walled city or was her confidence in the God of Israel? At the time of her decision to hide the spies, she had no guarantee that they would even listen to any plea she would offer. The decision had to be a quick one, but we can rest assured that the faith that propelled her actions was purposeful and deliberate. She had weighed the evidence of Israel's history. She had considered the future of Jericho. She was aware of the penalty that would come if the king's men decided to search her home. But she stepped out in faith. Her actions were far from politically correct, but they were a reasoned response to her trust in God.

Was Rahab saved by faith? Hebrew 11:31 emphatically states that she was.

> By faith the walls of Jericho fell down after they were encircled for seven days. By faith the harlot Rahab did not perish with those who did not believe, when she had received the spies with peace (Hebrews 11:30–31).

Was Rahab saved by faith alone? James emphatically states that she was not.

> You see then that a man is justified by works, and not by faith only. Likewise, was not Rahab the harlot also justified by works when she received the messengers and sent them out another way? For as the body without the spirit is dead, so faith without works is dead also (James 2:24–26).

Suppose for a moment that Rahab had professed her faith in Jehovah and His power, but had failed to help the spies escape. Suppose she had, instead, surrendered them to the king's men. Do we, for even a moment, believe that her legacy would have been recorded in faith's hall of fame? (Hebrews 11:31). How is it that so many in today's religious world are adamantly opposed to any suggestion that any work of faith might be a prerequisite to obtaining God's salvation? James 2:24–26 is not ambiguous. Hebrews 11:31 says Rahab "did not perish with those who did not believe"; but the Greek word for "did not believe" is actually *apeitheo,* meaning "obedient belief" or "compliance." Everywhere we read about Rahab, we read about the act of faith that saved her from perishing. She is used by James as the very example for our age that faith must be accompanied by works for resultant justification. May I repeat? Why do we in modern times have

Her actions were far from politically correct … a reasoned response to her trust in God.

such a mental block about the dual requirements of faith and works for salvation? I believe it is because we've been made to feel guilty by the doctrines of men. Somehow if I acknowledge that I must do something in order to accept God's gift of salvation, I'm suggesting that I can save myself; that my act of obedience is going to earn my salvation. If I believe I must do something, then I am negating the aspect of God's grace. Nothing is further from the truth. While numerous passages teach that my salvation is not accomplished by the perfect keeping of the law, or by any work of which I can boast, the Scriptures are also replete with passages clearly teaching that my salvation is conditional upon my obedient faith. Faith and works are, in fact, inseparable in Scripture.

So do I reject the power of God's grace when I recognize the condition of obedience? Did Noah, who "found grace in the eyes of the Lord" (Genesis 6:8), in any way make void that grace by his work in building the ark? Was Noah's work a necessary requirement for salvation from the flood? Was his salvation conditional upon a work of faith? When he exited the ark, do you suppose he credited himself with earning his salvation? His altar was a testimony of quite the opposite (Genesis 8:20).

List three heroes of faith from Hebrews 11. Beside each name, list the required acts of obedience that accompanied faith.

_____

_____

_____

RAHAB ACTED UPON HER FAITH.
SHE HOPED . . .

The hiding of the spies was just the beginning of a whole new way of life for this harlot-turned-heroine. Up to now, life for Rahab had been a succession of demeaning situations: cheap one-night stands—in general, a life with no light at the end of the dark tunnel. But on this night she would never forget, she dared to hope for an escape from that house of harlotry. She even dared to plead for the mercy of a God she believed could deliver her from impending ruin and destruction.

> Now therefore, I beg you, swear to me by the Lord, since I have shown you kindness, that you also will show kindness to my father's house, and give me a true token, and spare my father, my mother, my brothers, my sisters, and all that they have, and deliver our lives from death (Joshua 2:12–13).

Again there were stipulations. There were conditions of Rahab's salvation.

> So the men answered her, "Our lives for yours, if none of you tell this business of ours. And it shall be, when the Lord has given us the land, that we will deal kindly and truly with you." Then she let them down by a rope through the window, for her house was on the city wall; she dwelt on the wall. And she said to them, "Get to the mountain, lest the pursuers meet you. Hide there three days, until the pursuers have returned. Afterward you may go your way." So the men said to her: "We will be blameless of this oath of yours which you have made us swear, unless, when we come into the land, you bind this line of scarlet cord in the window through which you let us down, and unless you bring your father, your mother, your brothers, and all your father's household to your own home. So it shall be that whoever goes outside the doors of your house into the street, his blood shall be on his own head, and we will be guiltless. And whoever is with you in the house, his blood shall be on our head if a hand is laid on him. And if you tell this business of ours, then we will be free from your oath which you made us swear" (Joshua 2:14–20).

Notice the conditions clearly outlined:

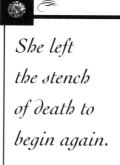

She left the stench of death to begin again.

- ❋ She was to reveal nothing of the spies' business.

- ❋ She was to bind the scarlet thread in the window.

- ❋ She was to bring all her family into the house with her.

Rahab knew that all her hope rested in complete obedience. She took no chances. She witnessed the miraculous fall of the city wall. Whatever was left standing of the house of harlotry had been transformed into a house of faith. The red rope dangling from the remaining window of the crumbled wall was a banner professing her life-changing trust in Jehovah. The same two men whom she had delivered to safety through the wall's window now delivered her to safety beyond that same wall, now reduced to ruins. Rahab left the burning city behind. She left the ruin of a fallen wall. She left the stench of death to begin again in God's Israel where she would come to inherit a place in His land of promise.

But Joshua had said to the two men who had spied out the country, "Go into the harlot's house, and from there bring out the woman and all that she has, as you swore to her." And the young men who had been spies went in and brought out Rahab, her father, her mother, her brothers, and all that she had. So they brought out all her relatives and left them outside the camp of Israel. But they burned the city and all that was in it with fire. Only the silver and gold, and the vessels of bronze and iron, they put into the treasury of the house of the Lord (Joshua 6:22–24).

And so our hopes today rest in obedient faith. We can leave a fallen domain. We can leave the stench of spiritual death. We can inherit a place with the people of God. Faith in His word moves us to keep His commandments, His stipulations for our escape from the eternal fires of hell.

SHE WAS HONORED . . .

And Joshua spared Rahab the harlot, her father's household, and all that she had. So she dwells in Israel to this day, because she hid the messengers whom Joshua sent to spy out Jericho (Joshua 6:25).

Notice the significance of Rahab: "Salmon begot Boaz by Rahab, Boaz begot Obed by Ruth, Obed begot Jesse" (Matthew 1:5).

So many are unable to forgive themselves of sins God forgave.

Rahab moved on with her life. When life literally tumbled in around her, she picked up the pieces and allowed God to put them together for her. So many today are unable to forgive themselves of sins for which they have already received God's forgiveness. This seems especially true with sexual sin. Remember, Rahab the harlot was able to dwell in Israel. We too can dwell in God's spiritual Israel (Romans 2:28–29). No matter how wicked my personal "Jericho" might have been, if I have been obedient to God, I have escaped! There is no condemnation to those who are in Christ! (Romans 8:1).

Do the Scriptures excuse lying in the account of Rahab?

_____

Is it ever all right to lie?

_____

Find verses of Scripture to substantiate your answer.

_____

_____

_____

For what was Rahab commended in Hebrews 11?

_____

_____

Does her commendation excuse any sin that she committed? What about harlotry?

_____

_____

_____

GOD LIFTED RAHAB

The end of the story of Rahab is found in the first paragraph of the New Testament. Could it be that the Rahab listed in the lineage of Christ is the harlot of Jericho? Yes. All indications point to her as the honored ancestress of our Lord. The Salmon of Matthew 1:5 lived at the right time to have married Rahab. Tradition suggests that Salmon was one of the two spies Rahab hid in the flax on her rooftop. While this cannot be proved, we do know that Salmon was a prince of the tribe of Judah. He was King David's great-great-grandfather. The four other women mentioned in Matthew's lineage of the Savior are Tamar, the unwed mother; Ruth, the Moabitess; Bathsheba, the adulteress; and Mary, the mother of Jesus. It seems consis-

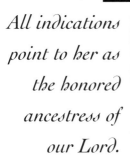

All indications point to her as the honored ancestress of our Lord.

tent with the context that our Rahab the harlot was David's great-great-grandmother. If so, all four of the women mentioned by name were women whose lives were vastly different from the stereotypical Jewish women we would expect to find in the ancestry of the Messiah.

What could possibly lift the harlot from the crumbling wall of the heathen town of Jericho and place her in the royal lineage of the King of kings? Only God. The same God who invites you and me to be children of the King!

Note to teacher: If you have it, bring a red cord or ribbon to be cut and used as a Bible bookmark for each class member. This is a reminder of the power of God to save and forgive. (You may want to attach a card to the ribbon citing passages about God's forgiveness.)

God forbad the rebuilding of Jericho in Joshua 6:26. What was the required penalty to anyone who attempted to reconstruct Jericho? (See 1 Kings 16:34.)

_____

_____

_____

Cindy's Reflections

Something Again

The tiniest piece of blue gingham
Saved from a small baby dress;
A remnant of a tiny pink bonnet
That once was my mom's Sunday best.

A workshirt without any buttons,
That old apron with orange rick-rack;
Just old sewing scraps with pinked edges,
But every small one was saved back.

Her eyes would light up at these precious remnants;
For each one she'd know some old tale.
"This one I made for your birthday,"
Or "this never did fit me well."

Scraps and more scraps of all colors
In that closet all bound up in bags.
She could untie them and fondly recall,
But to anyone else they were rags.

"Why do you save every scrap?" I once asked
When we went to the back room to mend.
"Each one was something I made long ago . . .
Each one can be something again."

"Something Again" is so pretty now
Draped over an old rocking chair.
She's long since left, but the squares in this quilt
Still tell of her wisdom and care.

There's the apron, the bonnet, and birthday dress;
There's a piece of that jumper I wore.
I cried when I fell on the playground;
I had stepped on its hem and it tore.

They once had been something of value
But worse for the wear, thrown aside.
But in those big bags, she redeemed them
And now I display them with pride.

She cut away stains and worn edges;
A pattern she'd carefully trace.
Then artfully piece them together,
And each fit just right in its place.

She bound them with batting and backing
And stitched them together with care.
Each tiny stitch is so precious to me
In the quilt that's draped over my chair.

I was a scrap in God's back room;
Faded and stained by my sin.
I'm glad He didn't just throw me away.
He knew I'd be "something again."

He cut away stains and reshaped me.
His pattern upon me He traced.
He stitched me together with others;
Redeemed me and gave me a place.

Once worthless and ragged and hopeless;
Now perfectly joined in His plan.
Discarded, but found, then beautifully bound,
So glad to be "something again."

CHAPTER 9

SHE WAS A REAL PRIZE!

ACHSAH

HER SPIRITUAL HERITAGE

Achsah was the daughter of Caleb, the man who was described as the one who wholly followed the Lord (Deuteronomy 1:36); the man who, at forty years of age, was one of two courageous spies who flew in the face of popular opinion and stood squarely on his faith (Numbers 13:30); the one who was forced to wander in the wilderness forty years because of the sins

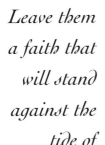

Leave them a faith that will stand against the tide of popular opinion.

of others and yet never lost his trust in the One who was leading (Numbers 14:30); the man who, at eighty years of age bravely said, "Give me this mountain" (Joshua 14:12), and, true to his purpose, he conquered the mountain.

Many of us will not be able to leave lots of worldly possessions or any degree of wealth to our children. But we can leave them a faith that will stand even against the tide of popular opinion. We can leave them the memory of a mother's trust that always wandered wherever God led. We can give them courage to conquer mountains for the Lord. We can now make deposits into a spiritual account upon which their souls may draw through years of their lives that we will never see, an account of per-

sonal prayers lifted for their spiritual prosperity, an account of faith that will be an ever present resource in the darkest days of reversal.

This legacy of a strong faith was passed along to Achsah. The evidence that Caleb, Achsah's father, was not a Hebrew by birth is strong and compelling. Notice this evidence:

Caleb is referenced as a Kenezite (Numbers 32:12; Joshua 14:6, 14). Kenezites were people of an Edomite clan of the area that later became southern Judah. When God commended Caleb in Numbers 14:24, He promised him an inheritance in Canaan. If Caleb had been of the lineage of Judah, this inheritance would have been automatic. The promise of this verse would seem redundant. (Note that this inheritance was not promised to Joshua specifically at this time.) Joshua 15:13 says that Joshua gave Caleb an inheritance among the children of Judah as God had commanded him. Caleb is set apart as one who received land as a result of a specific command of God rather than as a birthright.

Caleb likely became a Hebrew in much the same way Rahab did as he witnessed the incredible deliverance of Jehovah. His faith, acquired by his own observations, was the driving force of His godly life. God saw within him a different spirit—another spirit (Numbers 14:24). This different spirit controlled his decisions and secured his place as a prince of Judah.

I want my children to be able to look back on their "raising" and acknowledge that I was driven by another spirit, a spirit of courage and faith based on my study of His deliverance in Scripture. I want them to have a spiritual heritage similar to Achsah's. This will be the greatest family heirloom I can pass to them.

List the top five things you hope to leave as your children's inheritance—or a loved one's inheritance. Evaluate the validity of your list and tape it in your Bible so you can refer to it as you grow in Christ.

_____

_____

_____

Ask a teenager: "What five things do you hope to inherit from your mother or loved one?" Survey more than one if possible. How does this list compare with your list above?

_____

_____

_____

HER MATERIAL HERITAGE

Achsah inherited a portion of land. The south land in Hebron given to Achsah by her father Caleb was apparently dry. Achsah petitioned Caleb for springs of water.

Now it was so, when she came to him, that she persuaded him to ask her father for a field. So she dismounted from her donkey, and Caleb said to her, "What do you wish?" She answered, "Give me a blessing; since you have given me land in the South, give me also springs of water." So he gave her the upper springs and the lower springs (Joshua 15:18–19).

Caleb loved Achsah intensely. I think of my husband and our daughter, Hannah. I imagine her growing up as the light of her father's eye. (That doesn't stretch my imagination at all!) I imagine her making us proud as she marries a great man of God just like Achsah did. I imagine her asking her father if she could inherit some parcel of land or some possession that would make her life more comfortable. I easily imagine all of this, but it's extremely difficult for me to imagine her father denying this request. I am reminded of Jesus' words:

> Ask, and it will be given to you; seek, and you will find; knock, and it will be opened to you. For everyone who asks receives, and he who seeks finds, and to him who knocks it will be opened. Or what man is there among you who, if his son asks for bread, will give him a stone? Or if he asks for a fish, will he give him a serpent? If you then, being evil, know how to give good gifts to your children, how much more will your Father who is in heaven give good things to those who ask Him! (Matthew 7:7–11).

Achsah's request was granted by her loving father. It stands as a powerful parable of the power in our heavenward petitions (James 5:16).

Achsah's request was granted by her loving father.

SHE WAS A PRIZE.

Literally. Achsah was a prize.

> And Caleb said, "He who attacks Kirjath Sepher and takes it, to him I will give Achsah my daughter as wife." So Othniel the son of Kenaz, the brother of Caleb, took it; and he gave him Achsah his daughter as wife (Joshua 15:16–17).

Allow your sense of humor a small indulgence. Suppose Caleb had no takers! Suppose Kirjath-sepher just had to wait on the old maid who had no prospects. But it didn't happen that way. Othniel, a powerful leader, was all at once military conqueror and suitor to his cousin Achsah. (Both arranged marriages and marriages within families were common in Achsah's day.)

Othniel knew a good thing when he saw it. "He who finds a wife finds a good thing, and obtains favor from the Lord" (Proverbs 18:22).

What characteristics should a woman possess that would make someone consider her a prize?

_____

_____

_____

What three characteristics do you think godly husbands want most in a mate?

_____

_____

_____

Survey a few Christian men to find what characteristics they most desire in their spouses. Write your results below.

_____

_____

_____

SHE WANTED THE WATER.

I think it is interesting to note what Achsah wanted. She wanted the life-sustaining, thirst-quenching springs of water.

In making spiritual applications from Achsah, we should not overlook the New Testament analogy of Christ as our source of living water, our spring of life.

> But whoever drinks of the water that I shall give him will never thirst. But the water that I shall give him will become in him a fountain of water springing up into everlasting life (John 4:14).

> On the last day, that great day of the feast, Jesus stood and cried out, saying, "If anyone thirsts, let him come to Me and drink" (John 7:37).

As Christians we should look forward to our inheritance in heaven where the river of life is flowing: "And he showed me a pure river of water of life, clear as crystal, proceeding from the throne of God and of the Lamb" (Revelation 22:1).

> List two Bible passages in which water is used as a spiritual analogy and comment on each.
> _____
> _____
> _____

SHE WAS THE WOMAN BEHIND OTHNIEL.

> *He is described as a deliverer upon whom God's spirit came.*

In Judges 3:5–10, we read about a tragic national departure from God and righteousness. As a result of intermarriages with the idolatrous people of Canaan, Israel fell into false worship of the Baals. God allowed them to be captured by the Mesopotamians. In time, as was historically typical of Israel, her people cried to Jehovah. The first of the mighty judges, Othniel, was God's chosen deliverer. He is described as a deliverer upon whom God's spirit came. His hand prevailed against Mesopotamia, and the Hebrews had rest for forty years following the mighty leadership of Othniel. Mrs. Othniel must have recognized her husband as a prize as well.

> Who was Baal and what relation do Baal and Baalim have?
> _____
> _____
> _____
>
> ***Note to teacher:*** To further enlighten the class, assign a class member to give a short report on Baal.

If you were not raised by Christian parents, give insight as to how your appreciation of Christianity might be greater than that of those who might tend to take their faith for granted.

_____

_____

_____

If you were raised in a home where family members had been Christians for several generations, how do you overcome the temptation to be less excited about redemption?

_____

_____

_____

Cindy's Reflections

The Mountain

A mountain was before me;
A rugged, rocky climb.
So I began the upward path
That steepened all the time.

My burdens were so heavy;
With great pain I faced the test.
And I longed to turn back and descend . . .
To lay them down and rest.

"Don't look back," a voice would tell me.
"Yesterday is but a dream.
Lay its burdens at the water's brink
And forge this mountain stream."

And so the load was lighter.
I was given strength anew.
The mountain would be mine now,
For my purpose still was true.

But the sun bore down in torrents
Blinding me . . . I couldn't tell
Where the jagged rocks ahead lay.
I stumbled, then, and fell.

The everlasting arms were there
To catch me once again.
And a reassuring voice said,
"I understand the pain."

"Do not fear the rugged path ahead
Or shirk from the unknown.
For I will give you blessings
Where my sparkling sun has shone."

So the burden of tomorrow
I left lying in the sun;
And the prospect of what was ahead
Became a hopeful one.

Though the mountain just got steeper
And the sun ne'er failed to shine,
With each step my soul soared higher
And the mountain . . . it was mine!

My burdens still remind me
From that rugged mountainside,
That the shackles of another day
Are but gain when God is guide.

As I look down on green pastures
Greatest joys within awake;
For in truth, the tallest mountain
Is in the step that I now take.

"Give me this mountain . . ."

—Joshua 14:12

CHAPTER 10

THE PALM OF HER LAND

DEBORAH

Deborah settled disputes and gave counsel from her home beneath a palm tree.

THE TREE

Now Deborah, a prophetess, the wife of Lapidoth, was judging Israel at that time. And she would sit under the palm tree of Deborah between Ramah and Bethel in the mountains of Ephraim. And the children of Israel came up to her for judgment (Judges 4:4–5).

Deborah was one of a few prophetesses in Israel's history. She was perhaps the only woman military leader. She was the only woman judge. Though she was distinguished in all of these ways, she described herself as a "mother in Israel" (Judges 5:7). She was the wife of Lapidoth. We assume she alluded, in this self description, to her own biological children. If I am a Christian mother, then all other positions pale in significance. I might be a deliverer, a judge, or a military leader, but I am most importantly a mother. I like to think that Deborah was most proud of her role as a mother in Israel.

Deborah settled disputes and gave counsel from her home beneath a palm tree in Mount Ephraim. Obviously, she was qualified to settle matters of judgment because she received revelations from the Almighty as a prophetess.

Although our revelations are not direct revelations, I know several godly women who give spiritual counsel frequently from their homes. I know many young mothers who have benefited immensely from guidance given by a grandmother over a cup of coffee or during a walk in the mall. I know of marriages that have been salvaged largely because of good advice passed from one woman to another in living room discussions.

Tell about spiritual advice you have received from a mature Christian woman.

_____

_____

_____

We know that Deborah was the voice for God's revealed will as she sat beneath the palm tree. How can women today be used as God's voice of counsel?

✳ **Study**

The Word of God has life's answers. When a tearful wife sits on my sofa and pours out a story of infidelity or mistreatment, I know the Bible offers guidance and comfort. But it is only when I have a convenient recall of basic passages about this comfort that I can verbalize this direction and assurance. Daily study over a period of years is the only way to achieve a workable knowledge.

> List practical study tips (best times of the day, useful study tools, obstacles to avoid, etc).
>
> _____
>
> _____
>
> _____

✳ **Have an "easy" disposition.**

When listing characteristics of the wisdom that comes from above, James 3:17 says that wisdom is "willing to yield." Are you a person who is accessible and approachable, someone who responds with consistent kindness and keeps confidences? I know people who love to give advice, but are quick-tempered and impolite. These people generally find few takers. If I am to be a voice to other women for God, I must be respectful and gentle when approached. "But the wisdom that is from above is first pure, then peaceable, gentle, willing to yield, full of mercy and good fruits, without partiality and without hypocrisy" (James 3:17).

✳ **Be Fair.**

Notice James says that wisdom is without partiality. I must be reasonable and not blindly take sides before learning all the facts. I must always be willing to listen calmly, even to the guilty, before dispensing advice. When offering counsel I must compare the situation at hand with biblical teachings relative to it. I must not allow my shortcomings to color my judgments. If I have a problem being a submissive wife, I cannot allow this weakness to cause me to encourage insubordination in other wives. I must speak the truth and work to conform my life to it. No counselor is perfect, but the counsel I offer from Scripture is perfect.

❋ **My good works must reflect my heart of love.**
People approach those whom they admire. Most often, the ones who come for advice are people who have seen the goodness or have been recipients of the kindness of the counselor. If I have shown in a tangible way my care for a sister or a sinner, that person is much more likely to open up to me and trust my spiritual judgment.

I want to find a place under the palm and offer God's answers to those who may ask of me.

> Where does the New Testament address the concept of an older woman giving advice to a younger woman?
>
> _____
>
> _____

THE TROUBLE

Deborah's trouble was, at its root, the common problem of all the judges. The long awaited promise of Canaan had been fulfilled. God had commanded a complete obliteration of the heathen tribes of Canaan. (Notice God's instruction in Deuteronomy 7.) God did not mince words as He commanded this mass destruction. (Notice also Deuteronomy 20:16–17.)

But even a casual reading of the first chapter of Judges brings the reader to observe that Israel was content to dwell in lands yet inhabited by Canaanites. Their job of driving out, smiting, and destroying these tribes was half-hearted and full of cowardly compromise. Notice a few examples.

But the children of Benjamin did not drive out the Jebusites who inhabited Jerusalem; so the Jebusites dwell with the children of Benjamin in Jerusalem to this day (Judges 1:21).

And it came to pass, when Israel was strong, that they put the Canaanites under tribute, but did not completely drive them out. Nor did Ephraim drive out the Canaanites who dwelt in Gezer; so the Canaanites dwelt in Gezer among them (Judges 1:28–29).

Notice also God's extreme displeasure at this disobedience:

Then the Angel of the Lord came up from Gilgal to Bochim, and said: "I led you up from Egypt and brought you to the land of which I swore to your fathers; and I said, 'I will never break My covenant with you. And you shall make no covenant with the inhabitants of this land; you shall tear down their altars.' But you have not obeyed My voice. Why have you done this?" (Judges 2:1–2).

So the saga of the judges is a self-imposed judgment upon Israel. They left the tribes at least partially intact. They left altars standing and made covenants with the heathen. Before long they were immersed in the idolatrous lifestyle of Canaan. What began as tolerance of sin resulted in a wholesale forsaking of Jehovah.

And they forsook the Lord God of their fathers, who had brought them out of the land of Egypt; and they followed other gods from among the gods of the people who were all around them, and they bowed down to them; and they provoked the Lord to anger (Judges 2:12).

When open tolerance becomes the chief objective of society, society immediately becomes intolerant of the God who draws a line between those doing right and those doing wrong.

The book of Judges describes a dreadful cycle of sin in Israel. The Israelites made alliances with the evil people around them. The Lord strengthened one of the tribes or a particular king and Israel fell into captivity.

In time, when Israel cried out to the Lord, He would raise up a judge, a military deliverer, to war

But you have not obeyed My voice. Why?

—Judges 2:1–2

and win over their task masters; but when the judge died, so passed Israel's resolve to be distinctive and faithful to God.

> And when the Lord raised up judges for them, the Lord was with the judge and delivered them out of the hand of their enemies all the days of the judge; for the Lord was moved to pity by their groaning because of those who oppressed them and harassed them. And it came to pass, when the judge was dead, that they reverted and behaved more corruptly than their fathers, by following other gods, to serve them and bow down to them. They did not cease from their own doings nor from their stubborn way (Judges 2:18–19).

As Deborah comes on the scene, the oppressor is Jabin, king of Canaan. His warrior, the captain of his host, is Sisera. The oppression is indeed mighty and the thought of insurrection for Israel is intimidating because Sisera has nine hundred chariots of iron and has kept his thumb on Israel for twenty years.

Who would have imagined an ordinary wife and mother positioned to be the deliverer from such a foe? God would.

Read Deuteronomy 9:5 and Deuteronomy 20:17–18 and give three reasons why God wanted the Canaanites destroyed.

_____

_____

_____

How much are the words "open tolerance" used in American society today?

_____

_____

_____

What are some negative effects of moral tolerance in our society?

_____

_____

THE TRIUMPH

And so God speaks to Deborah. According to His instruction, she calls Barak to her famous palm tree. Here are her words from God:

> Has not the Lord God of Israel commanded, "Go and deploy troops at Mount Tabor; take with you ten thousand men of the sons of Naphtali and of the sons of Zebulun; and against you I will deploy Sisera, the commander of Jabin's army, with his chariots and his multitude at the River Kishon; and I will deliver him into your hand" (Judges 4:6–7).

What a break for Barak! He was told by God through Deborah that he would be victorious over the captain who commanded nine hundred chariots. His success was imminent. This was the God who parted the sea! Imagine the respect Barak would command as such a victor! Imagine the instant fame in Israel. But Barak's faith was weak. Hear his reply: "If you will go with me, then I will go; but if you will not go with me, I will not go!" (Judges 4:8).

What began as tolerance of sin resulted in a wholesale forsaking of Jehovah.

Deborah was to be the talisman for Barak. She represented to Barak the favor of God. He was willing to sacrifice the honor of victory to have Deborah at his side.

> So she said, "I will surely go with you; nevertheless there will be no glory for you in the journey you are taking, for the Lord will sell Sisera into the hand of a woman." Then Deborah arose and went with Barak to Kedesh (Judges 4:9).

Deborah, on the other hand, never flinched. She was decisive, courageous, and faithful. When the time came for the actual attack on Sisera's armies, it was Deborah who gave Barak the nudge. She was the great woman behind this man. She was the military motivation. Yet notice she gave God the glory.

> Then Deborah said to Barak, "Up! For this is the day in which the Lord has delivered Sisera into your hand. Has not the Lord gone out before you?" So Barak went down from Mount Tabor with ten thousand men following him (Judges 4:14).

When I offer people support through difficult times or biblical counsel for problems, do I remember to credit God and His word for successes in overcoming these trials?

The result of the battle is briefly summarized in Judges 4:15: "And the Lord routed Sisera and all his chariots and all his army with the edge of the sword before Barak; and Sisera alighted from his chariot and fled away on foot."

But the details of the victory are revealed in Deborah's song of triumph in chapter 5. It seems that God caused a great rain to flood the plain of Edom (v. 4) and the river Kishon to flood the battleground (v. 5). What good are heavy iron chariots in a field of mud? They immediately became a huge liability to Sisera's army. The horse hoofs were broken in the mire (v. 22). All of the splendor, the iron chariots and the prancing horses of the mighty army, were self-defeating when God decided the reign of Jabin was over.

Has not the Lord gone out before you?

—Judges 4:14

This song of triumph is one of the longest recorded songs in Scripture. It is replete with praise and glory to the Lord. The reader can almost hear the inflection in Deborah's voice as she rehearses in amazement the events of the day. It is almost as if she has to pinch herself to realize that this great battle has been but a simple display of God's might: "Awake, awake, Deborah! Awake, awake, sing a song!" (Judges 5:12).

Notice the closing words of her song: "'Thus let all Your enemies perish, O Lord! But let those who love Him be like the sun when it comes out in full strength.' So the land had rest for forty years" (Judges 5:31).

We would all do well as His women today to let this be our anthem in His army. May I be as the sun when God is marching on!

THE TRUTHS

1. Motherhood is the mightiest task of womanhood.
2. We can be God's voice to those who seek Him if we study His will and apply His principles of wisdom to all situations.
3. People don't care how much I know until they know how much I care.
4. The consequences of disobedience are far-reaching and devastating.

5. Wholesale tolerance—tolerance unrestrained by a standard—soon produces an intolerable society.
6. Decisive faith on the part of a great woman can generate great leadership in a man.
7. I am never great if I am taking the credit for greatness.
8. God can turn our assets into liabilities if we fail to use them for Him.

Give examples of how we can ascribe glory to God for our triumphs without seeming boastful of ourselves.

_____

_____

_____

Bring to mind one asset God has given you—has He blessed you with a particular talent or a sum of money? Has He blessed you with healthy children or a husband who is influential? Perhaps He has blessed you with beauty or athletic ability. Now write down two ways in which your specific asset may be misused and thus become an obstacle to faithfulness.

_____

_____

_____

❧ *Cindy's Reflections* ❧

Blessings of Keeping

Keeping scrapbooks and photos and memories,
Keeping late hours as seamstress and maid,
Keeping up with appointments, schoolwork and chores,
Keeping guard when someone is afraid.

Keeping food in the pantry and gas in the car,
Keeping warranties, coupons, receipts,
Keeping bouquets of dandelions, locks of blonde hair,
Keeping score when the children compete.

Keeping tabs on where everyone's going,
Being sure that my cell phone is near.
Keeping sleeping bags stashed in my closet
For those friends who always end up here.

But mostly just keeping on keeping on,
For life's about sowing and reaping,
When one day my home finds a place at His throne
I'll praise him for blessings of keeping.

CHAPTER 11

SHE
NAILED
HIM!

JAEL

SISERA FAILS

We recall from our earlier study of Deborah that God gave a mighty victory to Israel through Deborah and Barak. It is interesting to notice that in Judges 4:14, Deborah speaks of Barak's upcoming victory over Sisera as if it had already occurred. She speaks of the upcoming fulfillment of God's promise in the past tense: "'Up! For this is the day in which the Lord has delivered Sisera into your hand. Has not the Lord gone out before you?' So Barak went down from Mount Tabor with ten thousand men following him" (Judges 4:14).

Has it ever occurred to you that a promise of God is as good as done? I can speak of the judgment day in the past tense if I choose, because the pronouncement of eternal blessings on the righteous is as good as done. I can already call heaven my home if I am His faithful child because His promises are unbreakable. Hell is just as certain for the unrighteous and rebellious.

List other instances of God's promises being described in the past tense.

_____

_____

_____

So Sisera, with his nine hundred chariots of iron, had no chance of victory as he rode toward the river Kishon on that dismal, rainy day of battle. God had already decided the final outcome and no strategy, artillery, or degree of optimism on the part of Sisera's army could alter that outcome. Have you ever thought about the fact that millions of people who march in Satan's army today are fighting a war in which their defeat has already been decided? Satan controls the chariots of iron today; that is, almost all of this world's money is in his coffers. Almost all of the rich and famous people are his subjects. The captains of his hosts are respected and popular people we hear speak on television. We read about the successes of his army in *People* magazine. The voices from Satan's kingdom sound exciting and optimistic, even enticing. Sometimes it seems as if it would be a rather glamorous thing to be in this army with the iron chariots. After all, hardly anyone is serious about being in God's army anymore.

Name and discuss specific forces of Satan that seem to be winning battles today. (Example: Pro-choice advocates)

_____

_____

_____

Let's not forget that a dismal day will dawn for the forces of Satan. One day the chariots of iron will mire in the mud. All of the splendor and applause will come to an abrupt halt and King Satan will be forever put to silence. And let us remember that this defeat can be described in the past tense, for it is as good as done.

> Blessed are those who do His commandments, that they may have the right to the tree of life, and may enter through the gates into the city. But outside are dogs and sorcerers and sexually immoral and murderers and idolaters, and whoever loves and practices a lie (Revelation 22:14–15).

How can you be assured that God will win the war against Satan?

_____

_____

JAEL NAILS

What you are about to read is graphic. The details of Sisera's death surely were not recounted to my children in their early bedtime Bible stories. But God gives them to us:

> And Jael went out to meet Sisera, and said to him, "Turn aside, my lord, turn aside to me; do not fear." And when he had turned aside with her into the tent, she covered him with a blanket. Then he said to her, "Please give me a little water to drink, for I am thirsty." So she opened a jug of milk, gave him a drink, and covered him. And he said to her, "Stand at the door of the tent, and if any man comes and inquires of you, and says, 'Is there any man here?' you shall say, 'No.'" Then Jael, Heber's wife, took a tent peg and took a hammer in her hand, and went softly to him and drove the peg into his temple, and it went down into the ground; for he was fast asleep and weary. So he died (Judges 4:18–21).

There you have it. Jael opened the door of her tent to the weary Sisera, whose forces had suffered a humiliating defeat at the hands of an Israelite army much smaller in number. He was likely aware that not one single man of his army had escaped death that day. How small and alone he must have felt as he came stumbling to the door of the tent of Heber, the Kenite. Sisera

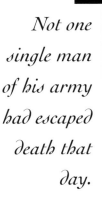

Not one single man of his army had escaped death that day.

must have known that Heber was an ally of his own King Jabin. After all, Heber had separated his household from his clan of Kenites and enjoyed a peaceful relationship with the powerful King Jabin. (See Judges 4:11, 17.) So Sisera was not afraid to entrust his very life to Jael as he stepped inside her tent and asked for a drink of water. Instead, she graciously opened a skin of milk and in feigned hospitality let him drink and then tucked him under the covers of death. Exhausted mentally, emotionally, and physically, he instructed her to protect him by standing in the door of the tent and denying his presence within. Then he fell fast asleep.

The Kenites were well known for their ability as metal workers. What did Jabin's army require that might have allied him with these metal smiths?

_____

_____

_____

Why do you suppose Jael gave Sisera milk instead of giving him the water he requested? (Hint: Milk's effect on one who is tired)

_____

_____

A FALSE SENSE OF SECURITY

Can you recall how good it feels when your head hits the pillow after an excruciatingly exhausting day? I believe Sisera had longed for a place of rest. Surely he felt a security in the tent of Jael. Have you ever thought about the spiritual implications of this false sense of rest and security that Sisera experienced? Surely there are many religious people today who believe they are securely tucked in that enveloping rest of which Jesus spoke in Matthew 11:28–29. But our Lord was abundantly clear in warning that just because we may think we are secure in our salvation does not mean that we are saved. It makes me almost tremble when I read the words of those souls in judgment who were resting in a false sense of security:

> Not everyone who says to Me, "Lord, Lord," shall enter the kingdom of heaven, but he who does the will of My Father in heaven. Many will say to Me in that day, "Lord, Lord, have we not prophesied in Your name, cast out demons in Your name, and done many wonders in Your name?" And then I will declare to them, "I never knew you; depart from Me, you who practice lawlessness!" (Matthew 7:21–23).

Pictured here are people who just cannot believe they are being turned from heaven's gates. They address Jesus as Lord. They are religious people who had expended much time and effort in their religions. They were teachers and workers. But they were said by Christ to "practice lawlessness."

"Wait!" we want to protest. "These are good people. How can they be lost when they spent their lives going about the business of Christ?" As heart-wrenching as such a scene is to our finite minds, I believe Christ logically answers our protests in the context of these verses. Notice His warning in the beginning of this discussion in Matthew 7:15: "Beware of false prophets, who come to you in sheep's clothing, but inwardly they are ravenous wolves."

You see, our salvation is not only dependent on our motives of sincerity, but also on our conformity to the will of the Father (Matthew 7:21). While we must do His will with fervent zeal and sincerity, it is His will that must be done. I cannot rely on what my pastor, priest, or preacher says. I am responsible personally to study and obey the teachings of the Word. The Bible is replete with warnings about the possibility that we may, even in sincerity, be led into false religions that lull us, like Jael's bottle of milk, into a false sense of rest and security. If I do not love the truth, I will fall prey to strong delusions that can be spiritually fatal (2 Thess. 2:10–12). I may die while asleep in the tent of a supposed ally who turns out to be the enemy.

What will happen to your friends who are resting in a false sense of security?

_____

_____

How do you think God feels about you if you fail to approach those friends with truth from God's word?

_____

_____

WHY?

So why? What possessed Jael? Why did she kill Sisera and how did she ever think to drive a tent stake through his temple? Theologians have expostulated for lo, all of these centuries on the "why" of Jael's assassination of Sisera. In researching these theories, I have most often read that Jael was simply a very barbaric and bloodthirsty savage of a woman whose shameless violence was just used by God to accomplish His divine purpose of defeating the armies of Jabin. While this may be superficially plausible, when I examine all of Scripture's revelations about Jael, I draw contrary conclusions.

Notice the superlative terminology with which Deborah, by inspiration, praises Jael: "Most blessed among women is Jael, the wife of Heber the Kenite; blessed is she among women in tents" (Judges 5:24).

Why would the prophetess call her "blessed among women" if she was a bloodthirsty barbarian? Deborah goes on to describe the death of Sisera in detail as a part of her hymn of praise to Jehovah. Would a dastardly act of sheer violence find such praise from the mouthpiece of the Almighty? I do not believe so.

Let's examine the evidence for a theory that Jael may have been acting because of a faith in Jehovah. We know from Judges 4:11 that Jael's husband had already severed his ties with his family, the Kenites. We know from Numbers 24:21–22 that God had issued warnings about the ultimate fall of the Kenites. While the Kenites ultimately would fall, we also know from Numbers 10:28–32 that they served as "eyes" to Israel as they entered the wilderness. This kindness was later rewarded by Saul in 1 Samuel 15:6. So there was somewhat of an alliance between the Kenites and Israel for several generations including the period in which Jael lived. Is it too far-fetched to think that Jael might have heard about, or even witnessed the power of Jehovah in preserving His people? Could she have even been aware that God had prophesied earlier against the Canaanite clan of Kenites? Is it possible that she might have even heard accounts of the great Moses who delivered the Israelites and started them on the quest to conquer Canaan, where she now lived? (After all, her people, the Kenites were descendants of Hobab, one of the in-laws of Moses as noted in Judges 4:11). Did she know about the blessings of God upon Israel in the wilderness? (Remember her grandparents could have very well seen the manna and quail, and the pillars of cloud and fire.) Could she, like Rahab the harlot, have heard of the mighty deliverance of Jehovah and wanted to be a part of His possession? I believe this is reasonable, particularly in light of the glowing commendation Jael receives in Judges 5:24–27:

Most blessed among women is Jael … blessed is she among women in tents.

—Judges 5:24–27

> Most blessed among women is Jael, the wife of Heber the Kenite; blessed is she among women in tents. He asked for water, she gave milk; she brought out cream in a lordly bowl. She stretched her hand to the tent peg, her right hand to the workmen's hammer; she pounded Sisera, she pierced his head, she split and struck through his temple. At her feet he sank, he fell, he lay still; at her feet he sank, he fell; where he sank, there he fell dead.

If Jael killed Sisera as a result of faith in Jehovah, she likely was acting in opposition to the alliance of her husband. If a Christian woman must oppose her husband to be on the Lord's side, should she oppose him? Defend your answer.

Read Numbers 10:29–32 and then 1 Samuel 15:6 about a kindness that was remembered for several generations. Comment on the possibility that Jael was acting on her knowledge of the history of God's people and upon a faith in the God who had sustained Israel.

_____

_____

_____

Discuss some things that result when we build relationships with non-believers by letting them see in our lives the goodness of our God.

_____

_____

_____

HIS MOTHER WAILED

> The mother of Sisera looked through the window, and cried out through the lattice, "Why is his chariot so long in coming? Why tarries the clatter of his chariots?" Her wisest ladies answered her, Yes, she answered herself, "Are they not finding and dividing the spoil: to every man a girl or two; for Sisera, plunder of dyed garments, plunder of garments embroidered and dyed, two pieces of dyed embroidery for the neck of the looter?" (Judges 5:28–30).

What a vividly tragic portrait Deborah paints in song as she describes the mother of Sisera watching through the latticework for her son's return from battle. I have a son. As I write this, it was only yesterday that I found myself praying fervently for God to protect him as he traveled icy roads from the university he attends to a speaking engagement in another town. When we arrived at the auditorium where we were to meet him and hear him speak, I breathed a great sigh of relief to see his automobile in the parking lot. He had safely arrived. If you are a mother, you are completely empathetic to Sisera's mother as she watched for his return and even as she imagined the spoil he would take from his great victory.

Sometimes life doesn't turn out the way we wish it would for our children. Sometimes, we've imagined great achievements and mighty victories that are never to be. Our job while we have little ones is to equip them with a love for God and a knowledge of His will. This is their armor against the foe (Ephesians 6:13). And then, when they are bigger, we, like Sisera's mother, can but look through the lattice and prayerfully wait to hear of their spiritual victories. May they be better equipped for the spiritual battles they will face than was Sisera on his day of battle.

Nine hundred chariots of iron are useless in a flooded plain.

GOD PREVAILED

He always does. Remember that nine hundred chariots of iron are useless in a flooded plain. Those who would fight against Jehovah may be gloating as they ride in their chariots and command their horses, but God is still in control. "'Thus let all Your enemies perish, O Lord! But let those who love Him be like the sun when it comes out in full strength.' So the land had rest for forty years" (Judges 5:31).

The elements stand at attention awaiting His command.

The waters saw You, O God; the waters saw You, they were afraid; the depths also trembled. The clouds poured out water; the skies sent out a sound; Your arrows also flashed about. The voice of Your thunder was in the whirlwind; the lightnings lit up the world; the earth trembled and shook. Your way was in the sea, Your path in the great waters, and Your footsteps were not known (Psalm 77:16–19).

Find a New Testament example of the wind and the rain being subject to God.

_____

_____

_____

Cindy's Reflections

Do You Really Believe?

Do you really believe in the promise of God?
Can you visualize streets of pure gold?
Can you hear from a distance the sweet angel tones;
Singing the story of old?

If you listen with ears that are opened by faith,
You can hear the pure water that flows
By a throne where the Father communes with His
    own;
And the light of the Lamb softly glows.

If you look through the tears to your homeland,
His voice of assurance you hear;
And you almost feel a soft hand on your cheek;
For He promised to wipe every tear.

Does someone you love live in heaven?
Someone who has gone on before?
Do you dream of that welcome from voices you've
    missed,
In a place where you'll part nevermore?

If faith cannot show me a heaven,
If His promise I fail to embrace,
Then I never can see it . . . I never can go;
For it's faith that reserves me a place.

CHAPTER 12

VICTIM OF A VOW

JEPHTHAH'S DAUGHTER

Known only as Jephthah's daughter, this maiden has been the subject of great controversy among Bible scholars in modern times. After reading Judges 11 and contemplating its message for women today, we are left with questions that, at best, leave us with a degree of uncertainty: Was Jephthah's vow a rash promise made in haste without any consideration of consequence, or was it an act of faith? Did he actually sacrifice his daughter's life in fulfillment of this vow? If he did, was this sacrifice of human life the right thing to do? Why was he commended in Hebrews 11:32?

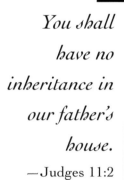

You shall have no inheritance in our father's house.

—Judges 11:2

FAITHFUL OR FOOLISH?

A modern American Jephthah would quickly find his way to the talk show circuit after sacrificing his daughter as an act of faith. He would elicit the sympathy of society because of the hardships he had encountered growing up. You see, Jephthah was the son of Gilead, a well-known patriarch of the Gileadites. But Jephthah was also the son of a harlot. He was the ghost in Gilead's closet. Gilead also had legitimate sons by his wife. These half brothers recognized the illegitimacy of Jephthah and made it apparent that they were better than Jephthah. "Gilead's wife bore sons; and when his wife's sons grew up, they drove Jephthah out, and said to him, 'You shall have no inheritance in our father's house, for you are the son of another woman'" (Judges 11:2).

What are some of the unique challenges of raising half-siblings and step-siblings in the same household?

_____

_____

_____

_____

Why do you think this situation is prevalent in America today?

_____

_____

_____

What can Christian parents do in the interests of the souls of these innocent children?

_____

_____

_____

Jephthah was rejected by his own family. So he ran away from the oppressive situation at home only to fall into the company of vain men in the land of Tob. (Even in America today, psychologists tell us that inner city gangs are generally comprised of boys who have failed to find love and acceptance within the family unit.) So Jephthah is running with the wrong crowd and there is neither a vigilant mother nor a firm father's hand to pull him from this bad company.

Look for statistics on the relationship between the decay of family in America and the increase in gang membership, and write down your findings.

_____

_____

_____

We may safely assume from Judges 11:3 that Jephthah settled into this vain lifestyle and became a part of the "Tob gang." It was only when Ammon made war against Israel and had the Gileadites "shaking in their boots" that Jephthah's brothers remembered the brother they had disowned. They knew that he was a "mighty man of valor" (v. 1), and they had hopes that he could return home and lead the defense against Ammon. So they implored him to return and be their captain in war: "Then they said to Jephthah,

'Come and be our commander, that we may fight against the people of Ammon'" (Judges 11:6).

Amazing, isn't it, how very little human nature seems to evolve throughout the centuries. Many today selfishly rebuff or ignore their fellows in deference to their own wants and needs. Then when they discover a personal advantage in befriending the same fellows, they find it in their hearts to make contact and even sometimes to make amends.

Jephthah reminded his half brothers how they had treated him in earlier days. He recognized their present distress and took advantage of the situation. Jephthah insisted that, should he agree to be their captain and should they be victorious against Ammon, then the once haughty brothers would be his subjects. They vowed to do so.

> So Jephthah said to the elders of Gilead, "Did you not hate me, and expel me from my father's house? Why have you come to me now when you are in distress?" And the elders of Gilead said to Jephthah, "That is why we have turned again to you now, that you may go with us and fight against the people of Ammon, and be our head over all the inhabitants of Gilead." So Jephthah said to the elders of Gilead, "If you take me back home to fight against the people of Ammon, and the Lord delivers them to me, shall I be your head?" And the elders of Gilead said to Jephthah, "The Lord will be a witness between us, if we do not do according to your words" (Judges 11:7–10).

A MOTIVE AND A VOW

It is noteworthy to see that with all of Jephthah's bravery, his primary motive for doing battle for Israel is not faith. He seems little concerned that he is saving God's chosen people. (In fact, he later becomes a leader in a civil war within Israel.) He seems unconcerned with the fact that Ammon has historically been a wicked nation. His motivation is power over Gilead. His reward will be ruling over the people who once cast him out. It is for this reason that I believe his vow was one of selfishness and foolishness rather than one of righteous faith. While it is true that the spirit of God came upon him (Judges 11:29) and that his faith was commended briefly in Hebrews 11:32–34, his vow was never commended and was unnecessary to his success in battle. God's spirit was already resting on Jephthah. God's spirit needs no incentive to accomplish its purposes. His vow seems both ill-motivated and ill-timed. He seems to have been pursuing power in vowing rather than in seeking God's favor. The vow was foolish.

Did he sacrifice his daughter's life? I believe so. The record is in Judges 11:

> And Jephthah made a vow to the Lord, and said, "If You will indeed deliver the people of Ammon into my hands, then it will be that whatever comes out of the doors of my house to meet me, when I return in peace from the people of Ammon, shall surely be the Lord's, and I will offer it up as a burnt offering" (Judges 11:30–31).

Jephthah was devastated when his only child, a beloved daughter, stepped out of the tent to greet him. She was a picture of delight. With a song on her lips and a timbrel in her hand, she danced toward her father, expecting a jubilant embrace. I imagine his body went limp as he realized the implications, now, of a vow he had hastily made in a decisive moment of his military career. He had likely not entertained the thought that the promised sacrifice would be human, much less his own flesh and blood.

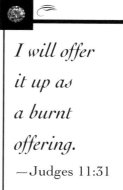

I will offer it up as a burnt offering.
—Judges 11:31

Jephthah was accustomed to the human sacrifices offered to Molech, god of the Ammonites. After all, the Ammonites inhabited a land just east of the land of Jephthah's childhood. He even mentions a false god, Chemosh (Judges 11:24), who was also worshiped by the offering of human sacrifices (2 Kings 3:27). Indeed Jephthah was all too familiar with this abominable practice, but having grown up among the Hebrews, he was just as aware of God's clear prohibition of such: "And you shall not let any of your descendants pass through the fire to Molech, nor shall you profane the name of your God: I am the Lord" (Leviticus 18:21).

Note also Leviticus 20:2.

> Again, you shall say to the children of Israel: "Whoever of the children of Israel, or of the strangers who dwell in Israel, who gives any of his descendants to Molech, he shall surely be put to death. The people of the land shall stone him with stones."

Note to teacher: Assign a class member to research and give a short summary of the worship of the ancient god, Molech.

He also had to be aware that God had never asked for or been pleased with a human sacrifice (excepting, of course, in the case of Abraham, in which he stayed the hand of Abraham, sparing the life of his son, Isaac). Yet he seems unmovable in his purpose to exact the life of his daughter in fulfillment of his vow:

> And it came to pass, when he saw her, that he tore his clothes, and said, "Alas, my daughter! You have brought me very low! You are among those who trouble me! For I have given my word to the Lord, and I cannot go back on it" (Judges 11:35).

KEEPING THE VOW

Scholars who have studied and written about the closing verses of Judges 11 have debated whether or not Jephthah actually offered his child as a burnt offering. Some have interpreted verses 38–39 to mean that he kept her from marrying and bearing children, in a sort of compromise sacrifice. (Marriage and giving birth were the high aspirations of all Hebrew maidens at this time.) But there is no apparent indication that Jephthah did anything other than the exact action he had promised as he readied for battle. The closing verses are filled with great lamentation on the part of Jephthah, his daughter, and her friends. It closes by assuring the reader that Jephthah did keep his vow:

> And it was so at the end of two months that she returned to her father, and he carried out his vow with her which he had vowed. She knew no man. And it became a custom in Israel that the daughters of Israel went four days each year to lament the daughter of Jephthah the Gileadite (Judges 11:39–40).

Research and find a scholar who believes that Jephthah's daughter was spared. Are the arguments for this belief plausible?

_____

_____

_____

WAS THE SACRIFICE THE RIGHT THING TO DO?

I believe not. There are many situations in which we may find ourselves having purposed to do the wrong thing. Sometimes in human haste or in times of misinformation we may even give our verbal promises to take courses of action that are contrary to God's will for us. In these cases we should repent of the wrong judgment in vowing erroneously and commit to a new course of action—the right course of action. A prime New Testament example is Saul on the road to Damascus in Acts 9. He had made a commitment to imprison Christians. He had most certainly promised his fellow Jews and his God whom he served in all good conscience, albeit erroneously. When Paul learned new information and became convinced that his purpose to imprison Christians was opposed to the will of the One he was serving, he changed that purpose and took an opposite course of action.

Foolish vows were kept in obvious rebellion to God's will.

We can see other instances as well, when foolish vows were kept in obvious rebellion to God's will. Herod comes to mind in Matthew 14. He, upon seeing the daughter of Herodias dance, promised with an oath to give her whatever she requested, up to half of his kingdom. You will recall that she requested the head of God's faithful prophet, John the Baptist, on a charger. Herod fulfilled his promise. But can anyone say he showed integrity in the keeping of the vow? Of course not.

Darius, king of the Chaldeans, pledged by decree to throw anyone who prayed to any god or man besides himself into a den of lions. You remember it was courageous Daniel who faithfully prayed to Jehovah. While Darius was smitten with regret for having issued such a foolish decree, he found himself powerless to recall it and fearful to defy it. Being under enormous legal pressure, he did the wrong thing and cast Daniel among the lions. Two wrongs did not make a right. God proved this in His mighty deliverance of His faithful prayer warrior, Daniel (Daniel 6).

Find other Bible characters who veered from their original pledges or purposes in order to do the right thing.

_____

_____

_____

How do you suppose God feels about those who should have changed their minds but refused to do so?

_____

_____

_____

If you have been forced by truth to change a course midstream, tell the class about this experience. How did this honest response to truth impact your children?

_____

_____

_____

FLEE FROM THE WRONG COURSE.

What about us today? Are there times when we need to swallow pride and repent of foolish purposes or promises? Surely instances around us are obvious. I have known of several people who have devoted themselves to religious doctrines and bodies. They, upon becoming members of such bodies, have promised faithfulness to the ideals and doctrines of the various creeds. These promises of devotion were made in all good conscience and the hearts of such people were always sincere. Upon further study, these people have come to the conclusion that the New Testament teachings are different from the doctrines of their churches. They have two options at this point. One is to surrender to the teachings of the New Testament. This choice often takes a great deal of courage. It takes the loss of a religious community they have come to love and respect. Sometimes it even requires an estrangement from family or an admission that parents and grandparents lived their lives in doctrinal error. This sort of change from an original purpose, you see, takes far more integrity and fortitude than staying the course of wrong.

Staying true to the course of wrong is the second option. I am thinking right now of a man who actually admitted that he knew that the teachings of his church were not biblical, even relative to what a person must do to be saved. While this man would make such assertions, he still persisted in this false religion. He had family members who would be disappointed and shocked if he left. He held a position as a deacon in this church. His pride just stood in the way of recanting at this late stage of the game. For several years, I prayed that this man would muster the courage to change his purpose and conform that purpose to what he knew was right. You can imagine my joy when I got a phone call one evening and heard the news that he had obeyed the gospel plan of salvation, giving up the religion of his past. I must add here that this man has now been faithful to God's truth for several years and has never been happier. In fact, he cannot now imagine compromising truth for any prior commitment.

Do we need to swallow pride and repent of foolish promises?

What about us? Do we make sure our hearts are always open to His will? Are we courageous and humble enough to change when we see our lives clashing with His Word? Can we recant decisions or commitments no matter how deeply involved we may have become in the ramifications of those earlier mistakes? We should all pray daily for the integrity, wisdom, and courage to conform to His will at all costs.

WHY WAS JEPHTHAH COMMENDED?

I believe Jephthah's decision to honor a hastily made vow, even when he learned it involved human sacrifice, added tragic folly to foolishness. But why then was he commended in Hebrews 11?

> And what more shall I say? For the time would fail me to tell of Gideon and Barak and Samson and Jephthah, also of David and Samuel and the prophets: who through faith subdued kingdoms, worked righteousness, obtained promises, stopped the mouths of lions, quenched the violence of fire, escaped the edge of the sword, out of weakness were made strong, became valiant in battle, turned to flight the armies of the aliens (Hebrews 11:32–34).

Why is Jephthah's name included in this list of men and women motivated by faith? If his decisions were selfish, why is he commended for his faith? Obviously, not all of those listed in Hebrews 11 are intended to be role models of character for us today. Even a casual study of the life of

Samson, for instance, convinces us that he was not the kind of man we hope our children emulate. When we look at Jephthah's story as it unfolds in the book of Judges, there seems to be little strength of character. Perhaps that is the real essence of what we learn from Jephthah. God took an illegitimate son, weak of character, outcast by his family, and selfish in his motives and won a great victory over an idolatrous nation. I believe that the key is found in Judges 11:29, where the Scripture says, "The Spirit of the Lord came upon Jephthah." Jephthah was a former gang member, a foolish rowdy rabble-rouser who wasn't afraid to stand up to the enemy if there was something worthwhile in it for him. But God chose Jephthah to be his vessel of deliverance. With the spirit of God, Jephthah could triumph. Of course, without it he would have been a colossal failure.

God took an illegitimate son and won a great victory.

I believe that the faith commended in Hebrews 11 was a faith mustered for the battle against the Ammonites rather than a consistent faith that pervaded Jephthah's life. I believe it was the one-time response to the spirit of God to become valiant in battle and turn to flight the armies of the aliens (Hebrews 11:34). After all, in spite of his weak character, he realized at the crucial battle hour that the victory was dependent on God. Even his rash vow evidences the fact that he knew that when all was said and done, God controlled the outcome. It is this moment in Jephthah's life, this moment of truth when he was blessed with God's spirit, that eclipses Jephthah's former life of wantonness and his sorrow-filled future, reserving his place in Hebrews 11. It is this courage in the face of the enemy that we can spiritually emulate.

WHAT ABOUT JEPHTHAH'S DAUGHTER?

After all, the lesson is really supposed to be about the *woman* of the passage. Jephthah's daughter was really the victim of the entire saga. I believe she was led to sacrifice her life as a result of a rash vow to God, a misdirected act of devotion. There are important lessons to be learned for the mothers among us.

Jephthah, the father she obviously adored, exacted her very life as a result of his grave mistake and lack of knowledge about Jehovah. He led her to believe she was making the ultimate religious sacrifice when, in reality, God was not impressed with this offering. How careful we as mothers must be to know God! I don't refer here to being acquainted with Him and merely teaching our children a loosely defined belief in Him. We need to take great pains to study His revealed will, to know what His requirements are, and to impress upon our children the importance of Bible study and humility before Him. We need, by our examples, to teach them total conformity to His will at all costs.

From my childhood I can recall my mother's humble words: "Cindy, if you ever find anything taught in your Bible that is different from what we've taught you, then you forget what we said and you do what the Bible says." This is what we all should be telling our children. In this way we will impart a personal responsibility to study His word and an accountability to obey God. This accountability will transcend their allegiance to us. I'm very afraid that there may be many mothers who will one day be filled with eternal regret for having led their children down an erroneous spiritual path while instilling a loyalty to Mom's religion rather than to God. I'm thankful for a mother who verbalized to me her wishes that I follow truth at all costs. Doing the right thing must be bigger than doing what we've always been taught.

Discuss some practical ways we, in our homes, can instill a personal accountability to God's will in our children.

_____

_____

_____

Review the lesson and make a list of lessons learned from this account.

_____

_____

_____

Cindy's Reflections

But I say unto you, That ye resist not evil:
but whosoever shall smite thee on thy right cheek,
turn to him the other also.

—Matthew 5:39 KJV

Doing Right

Give me not swift solutions
Or conquests in the fight;
But rather give me peace inside . . .
To know I've done what's right.

I may win a trifling contest
If I merely do my part;
But if I go the second mile
I just may win a heart.

Let me surrender all but truth
To show someone the Light;
And then if he should turn away,
I'll know I've done what's right.

Let Christ be my solution,
No matter what the plight;
For nothing's really settled
Until it's settled right.

CHAPTER 13

THE GREAT
DELIVERANCE
PROPHECY'S THREAD

And it shall come to pass that whoever calls on the name of the Lord shall be saved. For in Mount Zion and in Jerusalem there shall be deliverance, as the Lord has said, Among the remnant whom the Lord calls (Joel 2:32).

This great prophecy of deliverance was fulfilled in the gospel's grand proclamation in Acts 2. The great Deliverer is Christ. The great deliverance is that from the chains of sin and death to freedom in Christ. All of the stories in this book are just threads in God's tapestry of redemption. They are but pieces in the puzzle that, when assembled, is a portrait of that grand scheme. All deliverers foreshadowed the great Deliverer.

But just think with me about the great redemptive strides made even within these few accounts from the books of Exodus, Leviticus, Numbers, Deuteronomy, Joshua, and Judges. Early in the book of Exodus, God made His purpose of deliverance known to Moses.

I have surely seen the oppression of My people who are in Egypt, and have heard their cry because of their taskmasters, for I know their sorrows. So I have come down to deliver them out of the hand of the Egyptians, and to bring them up from that land to a good and large land, to a land flowing with milk and honey, to the place of the Canaanites and the Hittites and the Amorites and the Perizzites and the Hivites and the Jebusites (Exodus 3:7–8).

From a family of slaves, we watched Moses become the great lawgiver. The law he brought from the hand of God would prepare the nation of Israel to bring a Savior to the world. It would foreshadow in many ways the new covenant of that Christ. We saw the people of God settle in the promised land and we were assured that every land promise given to Israel was fulfilled (Joshua 21:43–45). As we bask in the fulfilled promises of our spiritual Canaan in the church, we are amazed at His faithfulness.

We saw the walls of a fortified city crumble at the sound of a trumpet, and from its rubble emerged Rahab, living evidence of God's power to change lives. We learn from James 2:23–25 that her rise from ruin to righteousness was dependent on her works of faith. The necessity of obedience, man's answer to the call of grace, is paramount in her story.

And then there are the powerful accounts of the judges. The lesson the book of Judges shouts to us is that God's blessings to His people are conditional. The failure of God's people to completely drive out the inhabitants of Canaan, as God had commanded (Judges 1), continued to plague them and tempted them repeatedly to corrupt themselves (Judges 2:19). God's plan of redemption requires not only initial entrance into the kingdom of God through belief and baptism (Galatians 3:26–29), but a separation from the impurities of the world—a continued sanctification (Romans12:1–2; 2 Peter 2:20–22).

From the chains of sin and death to freedom in Christ.

From the stories of the judges we learn that God's spiritual blessings are not forced upon us. Never has God forced people to follow Him. Today He lovingly calls us, but our continued freedom is dependent on our decisions to live sanctified lives. We can, as Israel did, easily become entangled in the pollution again.

In 2 Peter 2:20–22, what analogy is used to describe God's redeemed people who are again entangled in the pollutions of the world?

_____

_____

_____

Considering those you know who have left God's sphere of grace for this world, what seems to be the big attraction?

_____

_____

_____

Read Joel 2. How do you know this is a prophecy fulfilled in Acts 2?

_____

_____

Find one or more verses that teach it is possible for a saved person to fall from grace.

_____

_____

_____

His power was infinitely vast and glaringly obvious in every situation.

OUR ABLE DELIVERER

From the slave-baby-turned-prince to the great avenging in Deborah's day (Judges 5:2), one thing we never doubted was the ability of the Great Deliverer. His power was infinitely vast and glaringly obvious in every situation. God is always willing and able to deliver. Man today is rarely willing (Matthew 7:14) and never able (Romans 5:6–8) in and of himself. God doesn't require any ability to save on my part. Just the will. If I will to be saved, I can through faith obey, and the deliverance is mighty. It is a heart that is healed. It is freedom from sin. It is release. It is guilt absolved. It is purpose for living. It is the ability to see through the lens of redemption. It is a lease on life that gives structure to my character, my home, and my family. It is heaven!

The Spirit of the Lord is upon Me, because He has anointed Me to preach the gospel to the poor; He has sent Me to heal the brokenhearted, to proclaim liberty to the captives and recovery of sight to the blind, to set at liberty those who are oppressed (Luke 4:18).

Are you yet held captive? The mighty Deliverer is able!

Find a passage that tells us that salvation is dependent on the will of man. Compile all of the Scriptures collected by class members into one master list and discuss these passages in light of modern day doctrines of unconditional election.

_____

_____

_____

From which lesson did the class benefit most?

_____

What issues or particular passages were most helpful to class members?

_____

_____

_____

What aspects of the study would you like to see changed or enhanced?

_____

_____

_____

Compose a letter to the publisher or the author and suggest changes for later editions. Send to the address on the back cover.

≈ *Cindy's Reflections* ≈

The Stone

Once upon a time in a land not so far away lived a powerful king. The king was just and good and deeply respected by all who truly knew him. Because of his great wisdom in domestic judgments, as well as in foreign affairs, the king was extremely wealthy, having amassed an incredible collection of rare jewels. The king, being surrounded with every luxury and every imaginable amenity of the day, deliberated about the best way to display his jewel collection.

He could build a new palace in the royal city and place the jewels around the throne so that ambassadors who traveled from distant lands could wonder at the wealth of his kingdom; or he could place the jewels in museums throughout the kingdom or perhaps in traveling caravans that would dazzle and awe his subjects who otherwise might never be able to see them. But in the end, being the unselfish and benevolent king that he was, he settled on a plan unlike any other ever executed by any king in any kingdom heretofore.

"Yes, I *will* build a palace," said the king. "This house will be larger and grander and far more beautiful than any man could ever dream possible."

And the cogs began to turn in the minds of the royal servants. The excitement filled the throne room as they began to chatter among themselves. The chief cartographer was certain of the perfect spot on the green and lush mountainside where the palace should be built. The chief architect was already wandering in his imagination down vast corridors and into large elegant staterooms. The king's designers could already envision richly woven silk on massive walnut tables set with golden vessels. Why, within a moment of the king's announcement, this palace, in all of its magnificence, was designed, erected, and furnished in the minds of the ambitious group surrounding the throne.

But then the king went on. "This new palace," he said, "will be the largest building on earth. It will become home to all of my treasures. Inside this house I will place every precious and rare jewel. My throne will be in its inner court and I will dwell in this palace."

All eyes were fixed on the king as he continued. Looking at the cartographer, he said, "Search out the southern barren lands. Find a spot in the midst of those farm villages . . . yes, a spot that is accessible to the masses of common folk in The Barrens."

"But . . . but . . ." the cartographer protested. "In all of my travels through Your Majesty's kingdom, I've never seen a poorer lot of people than those of The Barrens. The men of that wasteland scarcely have either the resources or the ingenuity to furnish their homes and families with the essentials, much less even the smallest of luxuries. How can Your Majes—"

The king, holding his strong hand out to silence the growing protests, interrupted. "But that's just it," he said. "Having never seen a single house of grace and beauty, the new palace will surely be a marvel to the villagers of The Barrens. They will surely recognize the great honor I wish to bestow on them, a people heretofore destitute. Why, most of the people of The Barrens have likely never even seen their king, let alone traversed the length of the kingdom to visit my palace."

"But, O King," said the chief servant, "surely your highness will not *live* in that palace. I mean, you *will* maintain your residence here in this mountain, where you can look down at the beautiful and prosperous valley of Greenwich; where you can drink of the waters of the pure river that flows under your very drawbridge; where you can eat of the grapes of your vineyard and wander through your gardens and call for your musicians and—"

Once again the king interrupted. "Oh, but that's the best part! I shall build this palace, not for myself, but for the common people of The Barrens. They shall leave their hovels, their shacks, and their wayside huts to find shelter, rest, and feasting in my house; and yes, I will dwell among them. After being so distanced by both miles and means from me, I will give them a place at my table and they shall bring their concerns to my throne. It will be a new and glorious day in The Barrens!"

The words were no sooner spoken than they resounded through the valley of Greenwich below. The people of the valley looked to the mountain and marveled at the goodness of their king and sorrowed to think of that heavenly palace on the mountain with an empty throne.

E'er long the precise spot in The Barrens had been chosen. The king marked the spot with a massive slab of marble from his quarry. The stone was perfectly smooth and each angle was perfected at an exact ninety degrees by the king's masons. This was to be the chief stone in the foundation of the grand palace. In its smooth outer surfaces would be laid the rarest of rubies and the clearest of diamonds. The stone was a perfect cube, a cube so immense that it was a daunting task for men and beasts from the king's army to transport it to the southern tip of the kingdom. But, at last, the huge block was carefully laid in the spot ordered by the king. It lay in a most accessible spot at the convergence of two major thoroughfares directly in front of the largest market place in The Barrens.

The king immediately proceeded to complete detailed instructions for the building of the palace. The plans were most specific, describing every material required and the exact location of the kings' storehouses so that all materials could be easily acquired. All dimensions, colors, and even the furnishings were described in detail. The king worked diligently to complete the plans and, with his own hand, inscribed the invitation to the villagers to dwell in the palace upon its completion. Copies were made of the document and the king's herald was on his way to The Barrens to announce the king's plan.

A grand festival was to be held at the market place. At the time of harvest the villagers traveled from far and near to this large assembly. As they did each year, they brought their produce and livestock, meager as it was, for bartering. But this year, the villagers were especially excited as they made the journey. They were eager to hear the king's message to be read by the herald at the festival.

But what occurred at the crossroads where the marble stone lay was a sight to behold. Beasts of burden—camels, donkeys, mules, and oxen—just stopped in the middle of the intersection and sat down beneath their loads as if the stone were just too large to bypass. Farmers were heard cursing the stone and whoever had placed it in the middle of the road. Weary women murmured at the extra distance required to walk around the rock. In the crowded marketplace, conversation could be heard about *the rock*. Speculations were being made about who would have placed the huge and imposing obstacle right in the middle of their busiest thoroughfare. Various plans were already being suggested as to how to remove the rock. All in all, the villagers were none too happy about the rock.

At last the moment came for the king's herald to make his proclamation. He was announced and began to read the king's invitation:

> Hear ye! Hear ye!
>
> Builders needed for immediate construction of grand palace. His Majesty's cornerstone has been laid. The king's house will be placed here, in the midst of The Barrens, and you are hereby invited to dwell . . .

But before the words of invitation could leave the lips of the herald, the mighty voice of the masses seized the day.

"So it's the king is it? . . . He thinks he can parade into our market village and erect His grand palace right in the door of our market place! Why it's hard enough to have a harvest at all in this wasteland. But if our place of business is consumed by the king's palace, we shall have no place to barter. We shall have to make other arrangements. This means clearing new roads and building new edifices. Why, the king's luxury will consume our very livelihoods!" Their murmurs became outcries. Their outcries became insurrection.

The herald continued to read:

> His Majesty, the king, wishes to bestow honor on the hard working families of The Barrens. Rooms in the mansion are now being reserved without cost or obligation to whosoever will . . .

But his words were spoken to the wind. The village men had rushed as one to the crossroads. The stone was slowly being moved out of the road. The cursing was louder now. The villagers were spitting on the rock. Women were laughing at the herald as his lips continued to move, but no sound was heard above the maddening crowd. Children danced with excitement as they finally watched the rejected stone tumble down and rest among the debris of the lowland below the village.

The villagers, satisfied that they had made their point, walked proudly back to the market and finished their business. At the end of the day, they returned to their hovels and shacks. The next day they went back to the sweat of tilling the barren earth. They traveled back and forth to the market place on dusty roads to sell their meager goods for prices even more meager.

The corner stone was relaid. The palace was built. Its rooms were furnished and filled with grateful subjects to the north. And the king dwelt in the glorious house among his people.

> Therefore it is also contained in the Scripture, "Behold, I lay in Zion a chief cornerstone, elect, precious, and he who believes on Him will by no means be put to shame." Therefore, to you who believe, He is precious; but to those who are disobedient, "the stone which the builders rejected has become the chief cornerstone," and "a stone of stumbling and a rock of offense." They stumble, being disobedient to the word, to which they also were appointed (1 Peter 2:6–8).

BIBLIOGRAPHY

"Circumcision." *World Book Encyclopedia*. 1976 ed.

Deen, Edith. *All of the Women of the Bible*. New York and Evanston: Harper and Row, 1955.

"Egypt, Ancient." *World Book Encyclopedia*. 1976 ed.

Hobbs, Lottie Beth. *Daughters of Eve*. Fort Worth: Harvest Publications, 1963.

Lockyer, Herbert. *All the Men of the Bible*. Grand Rapids: Zondervan, 1958.

Lockyer, Herbert. *All the Women of the Bible*. Grand Rapids: Zondervan, 1958.

Spangler, Ann and Jean Syswerda. *Women of the Bible*. Grand Rapids: Zondervan: 1999.

Notes

Notes

Notes